DION FORTUNE AND THE THREE-FOLD WAY

First Published by The Inner Light Publishing Co.

This edition published 2002 by SIL Trading Ltd.

ISBN 1 899585 70 2
© Society of the Inner Light 2002

All rights reserved. No reproduction, copy or transmission of this publication may be made without written permission. No paragraph of this publication may be reproduced, copied or transmitted save with written permission or in accordance with the provision of the Copyright Act 1956 (as amended). Any person who does any unauthorised act in relation to this publication may be liable to criminal prosecution and civil claims for damages.

A CIP catalogue record for this book is available from the British Library.

Design, Typesetting & Printing by
Clinton Smith Design Consultants, London, NW3 2BD

Printed and bound in Great Britain.

The Society of the Inner Light has no branches nor authorised representatives and expresses no opinion on other groups.

SIL Trading Ltd is the commercial extension of The Society of the Inner Light -
Registered Charity No; 207213
Its aims and objectives include the propagation of theology and metaphysical religion.

DION FORTUNE AND THE THREE-FOLD WAY

By

Gareth Knight

S.I.L.(Trading) Ltd
38 Steeles Road
London, NW3 4RG

Other books by Gareth Knight

A Practical Guide to Qabalistic Symbolism
Esoteric Training in Everyday Life
Evoking the Goddess (*aka* The Rose Cross and the Goddess)
Experience of the Inner Worlds
Magic and the Western Mind (*aka* A History of White Magic)
Magical Images and the Magical Imagination
Merlin and the Grail Tradition
Occult Exercises and Practices
Tarot and Magic (*aka* The Treasure House of Images)
The Secret Tradition in Arthurian Legend
The Magical World of the Inklings
The Magical World of the Tarot
The Occult: an Introduction
The Practice of Ritual Magic
The Magic of JR Tolkien
The Magical World of C.S Lewis
Pythoness: The Life and Work of Margaret Lumley Brown

Books by Dion Fortune with Gareth Knight

The Magical Battle of Britain
An Introduction to Ritual Magic
The Circuit of Force
Principles of Hermetic Philosophy
Spiritualism and Occultism
Principles of Esoteric Healing

CONTENTS

1. Dion Fortune and the Three-fold Way — 9
2. The Arthurian Formula — 21
3. The Master of Medicine — 41
4. Dion Fortune and the Triumph of the Moon — 65
5. From Watchers of Avalon to Church of the Graal — 79
6. Changing Light on the Medium and the Message — 95
7. The Lady of the Lake — 106
8. Dion Fortune and the British Mysteries — 124

PREFACE

The chapters in this book consist of articles that appeared in the Inner Light Journal, house journal of the Society of the Inner Light, between Spring 1997 and December 2001. They have as a common theme, aspects of the life and work of Dion Fortune, founder of the Society.

Dion Fortune and the British Mysteries was first given as a talk on 15th September 2001 to the Wildwood Conference, Conway Hall, London, organised by Atlantis Bookshop.

1
DION FORTUNE AND THE THREE-FOLD WAY

The three major strands to the Western Mystery Tradition, using the colour symbolism popular when the Society of the Inner Light was first founded, were called the Green Ray, the Orange Ray and the Purple Ray.

The Green Ray consists of the nature contacts in the broadest sense, and encapsulates most mythopoeic formulations relating to nature and to the Earth, including Elemental and Faery traditions. The Orange Ray describes the study of symbolism and its manipulation in ceremonial or visualised forms, frequently in terms of the Tree of Life of the Qabalah. The Purple Ray denotes religious mysticism, a direct approach to the spirit, and the devotional way usually expressed in the West in Christian terms.

These three Ways can be equated with the three Paths that depart from Malkuth as we leave earth consciousness on the Tree of Life and visualise the three immediate Sephiroth in their Queen Scale of colours: the Green of Netzach at the base of the Pillar of Energy, the Orange of Hod at the base of the Pillar of Form, and the Purple of Yesod on the Middle Pillar of Aspiration.

The reason for this short dissertation upon the Three Rays is because Dion Fortune's whole life and work was based upon them. I was recently reminded of this when approached by someone seeking information about her, and whose preconceptions were so inaccurate as to be bizarre. They assumed she had started out as a pious moralist in the 1920's, had become an active convert to paganism in the 1930's, and by the time of her death was on the way to becoming a disciple of Aleister Crowley. In colour terms I suppose this might have been expressed in terms of watery violet, turning bright green before relapsing into rather murky grey.

Taking this scenario for granted the question put to me was, had she lived longer, what direction would her next work have taken? The answer to this question was simple. She would have gone on writing in much the same way that she always had - by a balanced exposition of the three fold way.

As in any practical occult work, there is always a certain cyclic action at work, based upon inner tides of one sort and another. One aspect may come more to fore at any particular time, but overall the balanced picture will be seen. One simply has to make out a chronological list of Dion Fortune's published work for this to be plain.

However, a little learning is a dangerous thing, and it would appear that a cursory glance at the 1920's titles of *The Esoteric Philosophy of Love and Marriage* and *The Problem of Purity,* were enough to give substance to my respondent's assumption that Dion Fortune began life as a pious moralist. Her novel *The Winged Bull* was sufficient to label her as a pagan evangelist in the 1930's, and an entry in Crowley's diaries recording some correspondence from her in 1945 was enough to put her in the ranks of the followers of the Great Beast.

To appreciate the full picture of a great occultist we have to take account of the many other books she wrote and their true nature. The 1920's titles mentioned above are of the nature of psychology rather than sanctimony, to which we might add *The Machinery of the Mind,* with an introduction by an eminent scientist of the day. Together with *The Secrets of Dr. Taverner* they reveal her early interest in psychoanalysis and in the medical applications of esoteric knowledge. She was married to a doctor with esoteric interests in 1928, and her principal teacher in the Golden Dawn, from 1919 onwards, was the wife of an eminent head of a large psychiatric hospital.

During the same period she wrote a number of articles on the nature of the esoteric tradition as it was currently being practised. These were collected and published in volume form as *Sane Occultism, The Training and Work of an Initiate, The Esoteric Orders and their Work* and *Avalon of the Heart,* rounded off by *Psychic Self Defence* and an early occult thriller *The Demon Lover.*

Moving into the 1930's we have an analysis of spiritualism in *Spiritualism in the Light of Occult Science* and a couple of popular booklets *Through the Gates of Death* and *Practical Occultism in Daily Life.* The major event of this decade however is her pioneering textbook *The Mystical Qabalah,* that spelt out the theory of occultism in readable and commonsense terms. The clutch of novels that immediately followed it, *The Winged Bull, The Goat-foot God, The Sea Priestess* and *Moon Magic* were written to exemplify in practical terms some of the theoretical principles expounded in *The Mystical Qabalah.*

Whether they were altogether successful in this respect is a matter for informed debate, part of which she initiated in a series of articles in the *Inner Light Magazine.* The novels were written to demonstrate certain applications of particular Sephiroth, Tiphareth for *The Winged Bull,* Malkuth for *The*

Goat-foot God and Yesod for *The Sea-Priestess,* whilst its sequel *Moon Magic* also has elements of the higher analogue of Yesod in the "hidden Sephirah" Daath. She was not an advocate of working directly upon the side Sephiroth, at any rate in her public works.

With their commercial requirement to entertain as well as instruct it is arguable whether the full demonstration of any particular Sephirah of the Tree of Life is attained by any of the novels, or even whether this aspiration is possible in works of popular fiction. However they may rate in terms of esoteric or commercial success or failure, the novels were an interesting and courageous literary experiment and have proved to be a lasting monument in genre fiction.

To appreciate some of the thinking behind the experiment we have to cast our minds back to the general atmosphere of secrecy that was very much a part of the Western Esoteric Tradition in those days. Israel Regardie, as he later confessed to me, was distinctly nervous at the time and for some time afterwards, of what might happen to him as a consequence of publishing the Knowledge Papers of the Golden Dawn. There is also evidence to suggest that Dion Fortune had a qualm or two as to whether she had gone too far in revealing esoteric secrets in *The Mystical Qabalah.* Such fears over such an innocuous book may seem little short of ludicrous today, but only a few years previously she had been bitterly attacked for allegedly revealing secrets in some of her early works. "Secrets" moreover that she had not been vouchsafed in the first place!

Nowadays at any weekend "workshop" one can sample magical techniques that were once held sacred to the innermost inner, whether presented in these terms or in the guise of some form of psychotherapeutics. My own first introduction to "path working" was conducted in most guarded Lodge conditions but nowadays similar techniques are the stock in trade of anything from day centres for the elderly to adult education classes in creative fiction.

Thus have the Mysteries progressed over the past sixty years in what is sometimes known as "the externalisation of the Hierarchy." This does not mean, however, that the Mystery schools are denuded of all power and wisdom. The greater secrets are concerned not so much with techniques but with the mythopoeic calibre of the material being processed, where indeed the secrets do not have to be artificially guarded for the simple reason that they are likely to be incomprehensible to whoever is not of the "grade" to work them. The pearls of wisdom are quite safely rolled before the snouts of the porcine fraternity.

The outbreak of war in 1939 put a sudden stop to the flow of publications, fictional or otherwise. In Dion Fortune's case this did not mean a withdrawal from the world or some kind of mental collapse as some have speculated. The reason is rather more prosaic, that is to say - paper rationing.

Even the *Inner Light Magazine* had to fold for lack of paper in May 1940 but Dion Fortune still kept writing away in open letters for students and associates, first on a weekly basis until 1942 and then, rather more expansively, every month. It has been my privilege to sort through much of this recently with a view to book publication.

Already published under the title of *The Magical Battle of Britain* is a selection from the weekly letters of 1939-41. It is odd to hear that some have chosen to look at this phase of Dion Fortune's work in terms of jingoistic patriotism. One can only say, as one who still remembers those times, that being machine gunned, bombed and threatened with invasion puts a rather different emphasis upon what may be deemed to be politically correct, whatever the long term merits of universal pacifism. Even so, the general tenor of Dion Fortune's approach to current danger, without rancour or vindictiveness, gives nothing that calls for apology.

Other writings of this time that are still to come include *The Circuit of Force,* which appeared between 1938 and 1940 before closure of in the magazine, and *Principles of Hermetic Philosophy* together with *Esoteric Principles of Astrology* that date from the monthly letters of 1941-2. Most of this work, it should be said, is of a more practical nature than the pre-war material. She discusses in some detail the circulation of force within the human aura, comparing western methods with those of the east, including tantrik yoga and the raising of kundalini.

Another initiative she pursued of a practical nature in 1942, evidently under inner plane direction, was an approach to the spiritualist movement, seeking common ground. She gave lectures at the Marylebone Spiritualist Association and wrote some articles for *Light* a weekly newspaper of the spiritualist movement since 1881 that is still published as a quarterly journal by the College of Psychic Studies. It also appears that C.R.Cammell, then editor of *Light,* was given the highly unusual privilege of being invited to the headquarters of the Society to attend trances at which Dion Fortune was the medium.

Her mediumistic skills were announced in the Monthly Letters in 1942 although there had always been a series of articles called *Words of the Masters* in the *Inner Light Magazine,* and in an article of April 1938 entitled *How Communication is*

Made she quite openly describes the technique of trance mediumship and what it feels like to the medium concerned, which is obviously herself.

The Editor of *Light* was not the only outsider to be allowed into the inner recesses of the Society however, for there are scripts surviving of medical doctors being invited in for trance interviews with one known as the Master of Medicine through the mediumship of Dion Fortune. These were of variable success. One early attempt shows the doctor concerned trying to trip up the communicator with technical questions and the atmosphere is plainly sceptical. Later interviews with a more open minded medical practitioner seem more promising and useful to all concerned however.

Some of these scripts circulated privately to those sufficiently discrete or qualified and the earliest date from 1921. It is worth bearing in mind Dion Fortune's long association with medical practitioners, since her pioneering days in psychoanalysis in 1913 through to her meeting with Dr Penry Evans in 1925 and their subsequent marriage. This regrettably did not last much beyond 1938 but it is an interesting synchronicity that in the immediate post-war years a very bright young medical student was generally regarded as likely to be her eventual successor as Warden in the years to come. That this did not come to pass is another matter..

This is a far cry from the mysterious correspondence with Aleister Crowley in early 1945 and the last year of her life. They had known of each other for some years, but kept rather distant relations, as is often the way with occultists of some reputation, who find no call to cosy up and join each other's groups. He did send her a fulsomely autographed copy of *The Book of Thoth* upon its publication but whether she returned the compliment with copies of her own books is open to question. The resemblance of the villainous Hugo Astley in *The Winged Bull* to the Mega Therion suggests that she was not entirely impressed by Crowley as a person but if he was aware of the parallel it would probably have amused rather than irritated him.

There is evidence to suggest that a rather sinister oriental group was flinging its inner weight about in the disturbed political conditions of 1945 and this may have led her to seek some advice from one who was certainly familiar in one way or another with various kinds of occult unpleasantness. There has even been speculation that an occult attack of some sort may have led to her death. Unexpected as this event was, it is not a theory I subscribe to, nor is it confirmed in the esoteric diaries of those actively involved at the time.

Indeed, by some accounts she seems to have been quite a bouncy inner plane presence very shortly after her physical demise, even becoming involved in helping to finish writing the incomplete *Moon Magic*. Some intermittent inner unpleasantness from an oriental source certainly went on for those sensitive enough to receive it, of which Margaret Lumley Brown bore the brunt, but it seems that all was satisfactorily resolved by August of 1946.

Contrary to popular fiction and film that sees occultism in terms of cops and robbers there is a very much more weighty and metaphysical side to it, which because of its abstruse nature, tends not to attract the public eye. Central to this is one of the first books that Dion Fortune wrote, on a high cosmic trance contact, *The Cosmic Doctrine* dating from July 1923 to February 1925. Until its publication in 1948 it was a text reserved as a senior study course, and was only published in full in a new edition of 1995.

The problem that one finds with outsiders trying to assess the work of any occultist is that most of the important work goes on behind the scenes, that is to say upon the inner planes, where few commentators have the ability to operate. Even if they have a certain facility in this respect they tend to be limited by their own esoteric horizons. Thus those not capable of appreciating the three-fold nature of the Mysteries, as expressed by Dion Fortune, will ever be lumbered with somewhat dim and distorting spectacles, only able to register the limited wavelengths to which they happen to be focused.

There is nothing that tends to throw this problem into glaring light as the so-called purple ray of devotional mysticism. Time and again one sees problems being thrown up by individual occultists or schools trying to come to terms with the Christ force. I use the term "force" with some reluctance as it is a very personal contact. However, in metaphysical and personal terms it is also a very potent force - and one that is not easy to deal with, by virtue of two millennia of historical presence in the west with many misapplications and distortions of it upon the way, by those who have sought to bend its power to their own institutional devices or dogmatic preferences.

The history of modern esoteric movements is becoming a fashionable subject in academic circles these days and I recommend to some aspiring PhD to attempt a thesis upon this particular subject. I have no time to develop it in depth but can give a few pointers to crisis points in the past where one can see the sparks fly. The electrical analogy is appropriate for such crises are just like a lightning flash - complete with rumbling thunder. They are caused by the same kind of hidden conditions, a difference of potential (electrical or spiritual) between the above and the below.

An early thunderclap and pyrotechnic display was to be witnessed at the foundation of the London Lodge of the Theosophical Society in 1883. The two poles between which the sparks flew were those who looked to the east for wisdom, as represented by Madame Blavatsky's protégé A.P.Sinnett (the recipient of most of the Mahatma letters) or the photogenic and charismatic Christian hermeticist Anna Kingsford.

Later we see similar sparks flying in the Hermetic Order of the Golden Dawn which led A.E.Waite to form his own more mystical group, the Fellowship of the Rosy Cross. One of the more distinguished members of this was Charles Williams, who went on to write some profoundly occult novels shortly before Dion Fortune was writing her own. I have analysed his fiction at at some length in *The Magical World of the Inklings* (Element Books 1990) together with that of his friends C.S.Lewis, J.R.R.Tolkien and the anthroposophist Owen Barfield. We find Dion Fortune herself involved with the self same spark generating problem when she had a profound vision involving the Christ and the Lord of Civilisation that propelled her in the direction of the Theosophical Society in 1925 and its Christian Mystic Lodge, despite already being a member of the Golden Dawn and having her own small informal but very active group. So hot and fast did the sparks fly that little documentary information has survived to tell the story. Suffice to say that the official Theosophical line at the time remained with a largely Hindu perspective of the Christian dynamic as interpreted by Besant and Leadbeater, and the Christian Mystic Lodge, of which Dion Fortune was then President, relaunched itself as the Community of the Inner Light in 1928.

The Christian element continued to be nurtured by a regular Sunday performance of a Grail related communion rite under the banner of the Guild of the Master Jesus. Dion Fortune herself also published a series of mystical meditations upon the Collects of the Anglican church.

So things continued in the three fold strand of Hermetic, Pagan and Christian Mystical celebration until the outbreak of war. It is true that for a number of members, any one of these three strands might be the preferred option. One of her stalwarts, an ex-military gentleman who wrote some fine pagan articles in the magazine under the pen name of F.P.D. was famous for his attitude to those he considered his esoteric and intellectual inferiors by his recommendation to "chuck 'em in the Guild!" However, although specialisation has its place, either in the beginning of an esoteric career or at certain more advanced stages, true adeptship requires that one play more than a one-stringed fiddle, and sooner or later all three paths from Malkuth have to be trodden on the long and complex road to higher consciousness in Tiphareth.

The post-war Society of the Inner Light as I knew it no longer operated the Guild although there was a genuine mystical religious strand within its workings, as one might expect under a Warden who had been educated by the Jesuits and whom some even suspected of being an under cover Jesuit himself! However, a very powerful Christian dynamic burst into the group in 1960/1 and one which was sufficiently powerful to cause many sparks to fly and various members to disperse and go their separate ways.

I had a very powerful experience of this myself whilst by myself in the Library. Suddenly, out of thin air, it seemed that Jesus, the Risen Christ, simply walked into the room. He did not do anything or say anything, and the experience lasted but a few seconds, but it was sufficiently powerful for me to go straight out and buy a devotional book to mark the occasion. It was a copy of Thomas a Kempis' *The Imitation of Christ* and I wrote the date in it. I have it before me now: 27th September 1961.

The group as a whole took a new turn as a consequence of all this. The old graded structure was abandoned and all reverted to the 1st Degree again. Members were encouraged to wear plain clothes or ecclesiastical cassocks instead of magical robes. I was prepared to accept all this as a necessary cleansing period prior to building up the structure of the lodge again. However after four years of things, according to my lights, remaining much the same almost exclusive emphasis on the purple ray, I felt a yearning for the orange and the green and came to the conclusion I would have to seek elsewhere to find it. So reluctantly I resigned. If you don't like where you are being led there is no point in dragging your feet and grizzling.

Anyhow if your dedication remains in the Mysteries, when one door is closed another will open, and "coincidence" caused my path to cross with that of a highly psychic and mystically experienced Anglican clergyman, who as a young curate had the daunting task of preparing me for confirmation into the Anglican communion. The result of the sparks we struck off each other led to the writing and publication of a handful of books, including *The Lord of the Dance* and *The Christ, Psychotherapy & Magic* by Anthony Duncan, and *Experience of the Inner Worlds* by myself.

Suitably equipped with what I hoped was now a stable foundation, I set about building my own lodge, with a structure incorporating bricks of purple, orange and green. How well I succeeded over the subsequent thirty three years is part of another story.

2
THE ARTHURIAN FORMULA

It has often been assumed that Margaret Lumley Brown was one of the principal instigators of that body of teaching known as *The Arthurian Formula*. However, recent research shows that although Margaret Lumley Brown was given the task of developing this material after Dion Fortune's death in 1946, the earlier initiative rests with someone else, who met secretly with Dion Fortune in 1940.

Confusion lies in the fact that esoteric reports and diaries of the time refer to people not by their names but by the initials of their archetypal function – and in the case of Margaret Lumley Brown and this other person these initials and even names were identical.

Margaret Lumley Brown joined the Society in 1942, when Dion Fortune immediately admitted her as a resident at the Society's headquarters. Whether this unusual act was one of kindness in difficult circumstances, or because her particular esoteric abilities were recognised by Dion Fortune, or whether it was a combination of both, we do not know.

Apparently Margaret Lumley Brown undertook a certain amount of light domestic work and cooking but in April 1946 she was relieved of all of this and admitted to the more withdrawn centre of the Fraternity, just down the road, where Dion Fortune had previously lived. She was told to develop her powers of mediumship as fast as she could with a view to giving the Summer Solstice trance address in June to the Fraternity as a whole. It had been the custom for Dion Fortune to perform this quarterly function in the past.

Margaret Lumley Brown was also given other esoteric tasks, one of which was to develop the Arthurian work that Dion Fortune had left behind. This she did, producing a number of lectures that she gave to other members of the Fraternity.

Who then was the original instigator of it all, who turned up in August 1940 and worked privately with Dion Fortune without even senior members of the Fraternity being told about it?

It does not take a great deal of detective work to make the identification. Her mundane name appears in some later work in 1942 that Dion Fortune conducted with some medical doctors in the field of esoteric healing. Her initials also appear in the earliest records we have of Dion Fortune's experiments in mediumship, in 1921/3, under her previous name of Maiya Curtis-Webb.

This explains why Dion Fortune looked up to this newcomer with considerable respect. Maiya Tranchell-Hayes had known her since she was a girl, and had been her mentor when she joined the Hermetic Order of the Golden Dawn in 1919.

Maiya Tranchell-Hayes is reputed to have been a walking encyclopaedia of occult knowledge, of powerful charisma and high life style. Some people even saw in her a model for the character of the Sea Priestess in Dion Fortune's later novels.

Dion Fortune had not been greatly impressed with the level of operation in the Golden Dawn as she found it, and eventually felt impelled to leave and to found her own group. Maiya Tranchell-Hayes, however, remained loyal to her original Golden Dawn affiliations.

In Dion Fortune's view the Golden Dawn of the 1920's had fallen into the hands of "widows and greybeards." This failure to attract younger talent seems to have reached its natural conclusion by 1940, when we find it stated that the Order to which Maiya Tranchell-Hayes belonged is no longer operative. Its last senior member has died and she is the only one left.

Israel Regardie, it should be said, also feeling that the glory had departed, and not wishing to see its knowledge sink without trace, had published most of its papers in America in 1937. However, revealing papers to the general public is not the same as continuing the higher practical work of the tradition. What comes across plainly in the records for 1940 is that an opportunity has arisen to graft the higher work on to that of the Fraternity that Dion Fortune had built up during the previous years.

In the pre-war Fraternity of the Inner Light, only the Lesser Mysteries were being operated. In a statement of intent made in an accord between Dion Fortune and Maiya Tranchell-Hayes and their inner plane contacts, the desideratum for the future structure of the Society lay in three Lesser Mystery grades (for the study of esoteric psychology, magic, and mysticism respectively) plus two Greater Mystery Degrees devoted to Higher Self consciousness. This is exactly what was developed in the post war years up to 1960.

The intensive work that followed saw the development of the Arthurian Formula, which provided the staple for Greater

Mystery work within the Fraternity for most of the 1950's, and the ripples from which in more recent years have extended out to a much larger circumference.

As Maiya Tranchell Hayes saw it, Dion Fortune was in a position to provide the conditions she needed to carry on and develop the work to which she had devoted her life in the Golden Dawn. It would also seem that Dion Fortune looked upon her as at very least her equal in authority and ability.

The two of them thus began to work together esoterically and, strange as it may seem, this fact was at first kept very secret. Even the most senior members of the Fraternity at that time were not informed about it until almost a year later. Maiya Tranchell Hayes attended ritual meetings of the Fraternity incognito, entering the lodge heavily veiled before the others arrived and departing after they had left.

The work that they developed together had three main strands. One was an approach towards the Spiritualist movement for a possible united front in the hoped for new age after the war. Maiya Tranchell Hayes was useful here as a close friend of Charles Cammell, who had recently been appointed editor of the Spiritualist journal *Light*. Another was a resumption of work on Esoteric Therapeutics that had fallen somewhat into abeyance after the departure of Dion Fortune's husband, a medical doctor, in the immediately pre-war years. (More detail on these initiatives will be found in the forthcoming *Spiritualism and Occultism* and *Principles of Esoteric Healing* by Dion Fortune edited by Gareth Knight)

The third strand was a series of scripts that came to be known as the *Arthurian Formula*. These formed a major element in the opening up of the Greater Mystery grades of the Fraternity between 1946 and 1960. During this period, senior members worked intensively upon the Arthurian archetypes, and even students of the Society's introductory Study Course, as I well remember, being one of them at the time, were required to read the whole of Sir Thomas Malory's *Le Morte d'Arthur* as part of their preparation for membership, along with Jungian psychology.

The *Arthurian Formula,* issued in cyclostyled form to senior members of the Fraternity, remained at the core of the Fraternity's work for some twenty years after its reception. From 1960 however, the work of the Society took a different turn, and moved away from Arthurian concerns. *The Arthurian Formula* faded into the background of forgotten things and languished as peripheral material in the Society's papers, a kind of vintage curiosity. Few knew of its existence who had not been originally issued with a copy, although by another happy chance I happened to have one, given me by the Warden, who was not ungenerous in feeding esoteric titbits to aspiring youngsters eager for information. It immediately had, and continued to exercise, a considerable fascination for me.

Under the general remit that he had given me, and possibly others, to draw on Society material in published work should this seem to be in the public good, I determined that one day I would endeavour to give the *Arthurian Formula* a wider readership. It was an ambition that had to wait another twenty years however, long after I had left the Society in 1965.

Although going my separate way, I retained cordial relations with those who ran the Society, and as a small publisher kept *The Cosmic Doctrine* in print for some years, and featured Dion Fortune related material in various magazines whenever I could.

I was at first able to encourage Arthurian studies only indirectly. This first was the result of commissioning W.E.Butler to assist me in running what was then known as the *Helios Course on the Practical Qabalah* in 1964. He soon came to take on the lion's share of this, and gave the fifty odd lessons for which he was responsible a firm Arthurian basis. This initiative subsequently went its own way, as all successful initiatives should, and in 1973 was relaunched as the *Servants of the Light,* under new management, but retaining Ernest Butler as its first Director of Studies.

My next opportunity came some years later, when I was in a position to commission the Arthurian scholar Geoffrey Ashe, who happens to live in Dion Fortune's old bungalow at Glastonbury, to compile *A Guidebook to Arthurian Britain.* This was published by Longmans in 1980, and has subsequently been updated and reissued by Gothic Image of Glastonbury.

The first opportunity for me to develop the Arthurian material myself turned out to be via a public lecture platform rather than by the written word. I was invited to present a series of public workshops at Hawkwood College from 1979 onward. The first was on *The Tree of Life,* the second on *The Work of Dion Fortune,* and the third, for the 1981 event, was *Arthurian Archetypes* in which I included material based upon the *Arthurian Formula.*

If previous events in the series had proved popular, this one turned out to be a sensation. It was on this occasion that I introduced ritual techniques as well as directed visualisations to a public event; techniques that I had learned within the confines of the Lodge but which, it seemed to me, could usefully be adapted to situations in the outer world. What else do concepts like "the externalisation of the Hierarchy" signify?

This was hardly a matter of giving away esoteric secrets as the most powerful event of the weekend's work was, at any rate on the surface, no more than a twilight recitation of the much anthologised Tennyson's *Le Morte d'Arthur*. However, the preliminary invocatory work upon the imaginations of all concerned over a couple of days, plus a little help from the inner, no doubt primed the pump. Added to which I was impressed to add a little spontaneous piece of my own at the end, with a view to deliberately calling upon the Arthurian archetypes. Perhaps I can best clarify this by citing my diary notes at the time.

"The working was a mixture of two techniques. The beginning was completely set, being a dramatic recitation of the poem by Tennyson *Le Morte d'Arthur*. Having already performed two powerful and demanding workings in the same day I would have been content for the evening to remain a simple reading of the poem, by candlelight and the evocative aroma of incense, as a kind of re-enactment of the way that the old stories were once told.

"However, I did have a half suppressed inkling that something more might be expected. This inkling had arisen on the Thursday previous when I had been packing my equipment for the weekend. Something suggested to me that I take a hunting horn. At the time I resisted this suggestion as there seemed only one purpose for using it, and I did not fancy the presumption of doing so, the responsibility or the possible consequences. However, I was quite firmly nudged to include it, so I did.

"Much the same kind of inner debate took place minutes before I proceeded to the hall to deliver this particular working. In the end I took the horn in my lecturer's box file.

"The poem tells in dramatic and graphic terms the scene of Arthur and the sole surviving Round Table knight, Bedivere, at the Lake after the Last Battle. The King is mortally wounded and commands Bedivere to cast Excalibur into the Lake. After twice failing to do so for plausible but specious reasons Bedivere finally does so. An arm rises from the Lake and takes the sword, and as if this were a signal, a barque with three mourning queens arrives to take the wounded King to the Isle of Avilion on the inner planes.

The poem makes the point that Bedivere now, as sole remaining knight, holds within himself the whole Round Table. The last words of the King are that Bedivere should pray for him. "It then became plain what I should do. I instructed all present to identify with the Round Table and to pray for the King. One was quickly aware that a great Round Table had formed on the astral, within the room, seeming almost as solid as physical wood, extending to the very seats of all present."

"I then took the horn and blew three long blasts."

"As soon as I had done so it seemed as if, on the astral, great doors opened in the West, together with a waft of sea air, and even spray. A mighty figure of the King came through the doors, crowned, with short golden beard, robed, and with the great hilt of the sword Excalibur very prominent, impressive with its jewelled work, and in its mighty runed scabbard."

"With the King came Guenevere, Lancelot, Gawain, Tristram and all the knights and ladies. Larger than life, they took up their positions about the Table Round. In the centre rose a column of incense smoke with astral rainbow colours manifesting the powers of the Grail, the Cauldron, Merlin and Nimué."

"To my surprise, and I was seated in the East, the great throne of the King with the Queen's beside it, built up in the West."

"The power within the room was intensely strong, so much so that the small table altar with the two candles and incense burner upon it seemed to be wavering up and down as in a heat haze."

"I decided to let these powers continue running overnight and therefore suggested that all present left quietly and independently in their own time."

There was to be, however, a further piece of action, for an occultist of some ability and experience seated in the west, seemingly became overshadowed with the archetype of the King. When all had left she felt impelled to come to the central altar and there present a message from a source that plainly was not her own, in a quite uncharacteristically imperious manner:

"You have done well, priest. As a result of this work new doors will open for you. A door has been opened that will not again be shut. A lamp has been lit that has for too long been extinguished."

This brings to mind that in magical work of any depth or significance, all is not over when the participants disperse, but currents and forces that have been set in motion, bound up into vortices, will have an effect upon inner and outer planes for some time to come. This may be felt in immediate personal terms, in dawning realisations, required actions and subliminal pressures. To quote once again from my notes at the time:

"Who we mean when we say "the King" must be left to intellectual conjecture. Whoever the original Arthur was, however, whether fifth century Roman-Briton or the Titanic god Albion, the living experience of the contact was one of reality. Call him "redeemed archetype" if one wishes, the reality is the King lives! Long live the King!"

"Having arrived home, with the realisation that the contact had been with the King, I received a telephone call from one who had been present, to say that the following message had been received from an inner source and seemed important:

"The sword is unsheathed and should be kept on the altar in that way. "

It became immediately apparent to me that the implication of this was that the forces of the King were abroad in the land and that all who had been present should be informed of the matter. I accordingly made arrangements for those who had been present to be so informed. Until this had been achieved I was under intense subliminal pressure - the neck and shoulders tense as if carrying a great yoke. As the word spread so this condition eased."

Another report of the time by one of those present, which is almost in itself in the category of a "received communication", gives a good idea as to what may be meant when we talk about Arthurian archetypes, and the consequences and responsibilities associated with them.

"The rite still goes on. The working at Hawkwood was only

the beginning. The working of the rite now goes on in our daily lives."

"In the King meet the deepest roots of the earth of Logres, roots that go back to the beginning of the race and the beginning of the land, with highest Christian and Pagan aspirations. The sword lies drawn upon the altar of the earth of Britain to achieve once more the land of Logres under the King. The sword was brought back from the sea by the King and is the direct, naked magical power of the King working as in earth."

"The King serves under Christ. He is the greatest servant of all. His return means a great revolutionary stride forward in the spiritual destiny of these islands. All the healing power of the old kings is concentrated in Arthur. He has returned to heal the land of Britain in its time of need, and his rule will be conducted at the Round Table. He seems to say that the destiny of Logres is that of spiritual leadership of Europe. Britain is the islands to the north, which were considered of old to be Holy Islands. The myths of Joseph of Arimathea, Atlantis and the possibility that the Lord Himself, as a child, came to these lands, lies deep within the racial consciousness, as well as the pagan mythology of the matter of Britain."

"The King seems to say that we may not yet realise the power at our disposal with the sword lying on the altar, but it will be made clear. I saw the sword lying north to south across Britain with its hilt east to west. It became a Rose Cross. The King now seems to be dwelling within the atmosphere of the earth of Britain. He says: "Deep, deep rooted is the power I bring. High, high is the aspiration for the achievement of Logres. Great is the responsibility of those who are chosen." Wherever we go the power of the Sword is with us. We take it with us. "This achievement of Logres will not be realised without conflict. The present disturbances (written 1981. Ed) are the natural result of a great input of power into the racial unconsciousness by the return of the King. It is like the first stages of an initiation, which can be painful, but which lead to a greater personal realisation and peace. So it is with the land of Britain, with this great power surging through it and throwing up injustice and resentments that have been suppressed too long. The troubles will pass and these isles will once again take up their rightful destiny as one of the great spiritual centres of the earth. Britain will be transformed into Logres under Arthur. At first I thought that the archetype of Arthur would be viewed as an amalgam of all the noble aspirations of the people of Britain. But I now feel that we are the body of Arthur, or at least his arm, which wields the sword."

"After the achieving of Logres there will be a further transformation as the Grail is achieved and the whole earth is taken up into God as the New Jerusalem."

This report was from John Matthews, who since those days has gone on to become a leading authority upon the Arthurian tradition and the Grail, with many books to his credit, and along with Caitlin Matthews has founded *Hallowquest,* an organisation with an international workshop and lecture programme, which still meets annually at Hawkwood.

As to the regally delivered announcement about new doors opening as a consequence of this work, I was very soon after commissioned to write a book upon the Arthurian legend, which was published two years later, in 1983, as *The Secret Tradition in Arthurian Legend.* In this I was able to fulfil my long held ambition to put as much as I could of the original *Arthurian Formula* into the public domain.

This I acknowledged in the Preface, and dedicated the book "to the memory of Violet Mary Firth, true flower of the Earth of Avalon, who blaized the trail in this Quest, and to the company of Hawkwood who followed it." A similar tribute to Margaret Lumley Brown came in the dedication of the following volume *The Rose Cross and the Goddess* (called in an American revised edition *Evoking the Goddess*) - which was culled from later workshops in the series, based upon the Mysteries of Isis and the 17th century Rosicrucian tradition.

Eventually the public workshops suffered from their own success and became over-crowded and a little too hot to handle on a public basis, but by then I had developed a private group to carry on the work with trained and tested personal students. There are limits to how far the powers of the lodge can be externalised.

The Arthurian work is, however, multifaceted, and public and private work upon it goes on in various directions, as indeed it always has. The torch is passed along from one generation to another. Thus this work that I did in the 1980's was directly inspired by the work of the higher grades of the Society of the Inner Light in the 1950's, which was based in turn upon what Dion Fortune and Maiya Tranchell Hayes had been putting together in the 1940's, whose roots are plainly to be seen in Dion Fortune's contacts at Glastonbury in the 1920's and Guild work in London in the 1930's.

In latter years I have also found this line of work to be of particular interest in France, where I have lectured and given guided visualisations to selected groups. As part and parcel of this *The Secret Tradition in Arthurian Legend* is now available in the French language and the Italian. By a quirk of the economics of the publishing industry it is, ironically, no longer published in Britain, but English language publication has been taken up in America by Weisers, who also have a stake in Watkins occult bookshop in London, so copies of the work should remain available in its country of origin.

In all of this, what gives me particular pleasure is that the *Arthurian Formula* has now been reproduced in its original form, and made available as a booklet, if only for limited circulation, by the Society of the Inner Light, from whence it first originated.

It may therefore be appropriate if I take the opportunity, in welcoming this long delayed resurrection, to make a few remarks about its content. It may be new to many readers but it has been a familiar source of information and inspiration to me for something like forty years, and so my long matured reflections may prove of some value.

I have taken some of its recommendations very much to heart. For instance, it says in the opening words of its Foreword: "There is no waste of time in considering the bearing of scholarship upon the study of the Mysteries in general and, in particular, the Arthurian Legends of which the Grail forms a part."

In this respect I have taken it at its word, and have spent seven years, since early retirement afforded me the time, studying French at the University of London, with a particular eye to the medieval period. Much of the original material of "the Matter of Britain" happens, for historical reasons, to be written in Old French. This is the language of the first Arthurian romancier, Chrétien de Troyes, and of the prose and poetry of the originals drawn upon by our 15th century translator of genius, Sir Thomas Malory.

Even so, this is little more than scratching the surface, for like a great range of mountains, scaling one height only reveals yet more. Thus medieval Arabic, the Occitan language of Southern France, and ancient Welsh and even Persian, would also have their part to play in a deeper analysis of sources. However, as the *Arthurian Formula* makes plain, at root we have to go back to lost Atlantis, and there are no written sources or language schools that can be of much help to us there.

Atlantis was, of course, always a keen interest of Margaret Lumley Brown, and as we described in *Pythoness, the Life and Work of Margaret Lumley Brown* (Sun Chalice, 2000), she closely followed the adventures of Colonel Fawcett in his attempts to discover evidence of this civilisation in South America, encouraged in his quest by Rider Haggard. We know that she had written to him in the first instance as a result of dreams or visions she had had that seemed to be of Atlantean origin.

There is a persistence to this legend, despite scientific doubts of its validity. It is to be found in the deeper teachers of esoteric lore, including H.P.Blavatsky and Rudolf Steiner. Dion Fortune also devotes a chapter to the subject in her early book on Glastonbury *Avalon of the Heart,* so she too was inclined toward the legend long before she met Margaret Lumley Brown. Furthermore, the mediation records in the Society's archives, most of which have been issued to members as study papers, demonstrate a strong and constant commitment by inner plane teachers to the existence and importance of the ancient civilisations of legend. Much of the appeal of some of Tolkien's works, particularly those relating to *The Silmarillion,* stem, to my mind, from unconscious memories of these legendary times, as I have analysed to some degree in *The Magical World of the Inklings* and *The Magical World of J.R.R. Tolkien*..

In the beginning of Part 3 of the *Arthurian Formula*, these ancient origins are staunchly proclaimed:. "First of all disabuse your minds of 'historicity' . The Tradition is that the Legend is a Mystery Tale brought over from Atlantis - a tale which exists in many forms and many lands but which has such a strongly developed British form that we are justified in counting it among the esoteric Mysteries of these Islands."

Hence in writing *The Secret Tradition in Arthurian Legend* I found no alternative but to nail my colours to the mast and declare in the Foreword that "Much of this material relates to the 'Atlantean' tradition and takes its validity for granted.... Those who choose not to believe it may find much of this book of questionable validity but I fear I have come far enough along the road of occult research to realise that there comes a time when it is too limiting to try to write within the framework of assumptions imposed by the current intellectual establishment." This stuck in the craw of one or two more conventional reviewers but this was only to be expected. Not, I should say, that I do not respect genuine scholarship. I simply count myself fortunate that I am not dependent on making a living from it. I am thus at liberty to believe and write what I choose, trusting to intuition as much as to intellect, and also to the information provided by communicators and mediators whom I have come to trust. Not of course that any mediated material can be guaranteed as error free.

Thus there are one or two errors of fact that appear both in the *Arthurian Formula* and in my taking of information from it for my book. One of these is a certain misunderstanding of the difference between "troubadours" and "trouvères". In the *Arthurian Formula* we get the impression that the latter are "esoteric" equivalents of the former. In fact it is generally agreed that the difference is rather one of geography and language: troubadours coming from the south and speaking Occitan, and trouvères coming, a little later, from the north and speaking Old French.

However, there is a certain split in their function as the troubadours tended to write the love lyric, in praise of the lady, whilst the trouvères introduced the more narrative element of Arthurian story. In this respect trouvères might be regarded as potentially more esoteric in content, as purveyors of the ancient esoteric legends. However the troubadour's devotion to the lady, by extension becomes a worship of the divine feminine, which may be regarded as equally esoteric, but after another manner. There was also considerable variation between the knowledge, technique and aims of the many individuals concerned, so all were not as esoteric or divinely inspired as we moderns may tend to think.

Although in these 12th and 13th century studies we are only dealing with a halfway house, a study of the period in some detail does bring its rewards. This is in line with another statement in the *Arthurian Formula* immediately after the paragraph just quoted: "Like all esoteric Mysteries, the Legend develops with the souls it trains and is not intended to be static either in psychology or in geography. Its 'countries' and 'events' are those of the soul itself..." It follows that it can therefore be very rewarding, if we take the trouble, to view this country of the soul through 12th century as well as 20th century eyes. The material obviously meant a great deal to them, so much so as to suggest that by some law of cycles, astrological or otherwise, the conditions of their society struck a powerful resonance with the legendary Atlantean times. The particular interest that we have in it today likewise suggests that echoes of this resonance are potentially applicable to us.

The power of the stories remains very potent. This is sometimes revealed by synchronicities when working with them. Thus in conducting a visualisation in New York upon the storm scene in *Yvain, or the Lady of the Fountain* the sky blackened over and a freak storm ensued at the same time. More recently at a conference in Lampeter when I spoke of Eleanor of Aquitaine and her Courts of Love, and how they had been sparked off by Henry II's affair with Rosamund Clifford, a large colour picture of both ladies appeared on the front page of *The Guardian* that morning. It is of course not very often that 12th century ladies feature on the front pages of 20th century newspapers, but was sparked on this occasion by the controversial sale of a pre-Raphaelite painting. The trouble with synchronicities is that, like corn circles, they seem to occur at complete random unpredictability. They also seem, in themselves, of little consequence, apart perhaps from indication that parallel events to the outer celebration are taking place upon the inner planes. This is the difference, I suppose, between "contacted" and non-contacted esoteric work.

Eleanor and Rosamund are of course not characters in Arthurian legend but historical personalities about whom a certain historical and romantic charisma has developed relating to this lore. This is another facet of the tradition that has been borne in upon me with continued and increasing force. It manifests in a fascination with a particular period of Crusader studies, relating to the 3rd Crusade, in which Eleanor of Aquitaine's favourite son, Richard Coeur de Lion, was directly involved, together with her grandson Henry II of Champagne, whose mother, Eleanor's daughter, was Marie, the patroness of Chrétien de Troyes. Henry II of Champagne became ruler of the Crusader Kingdom of Jerusalem, a short lived rival to the heirs of the family of Lusignan, who founded a royal dynasty in Cyprus and claimed descent from the world of Faery.

This idea of being descended from the faery Melusine, together with the belief that Jerusalem was centre of the world, may seem bizarre to worldly modern eyes, but that which is universally believed in any epoch pertains to the real in some degree, and we find a strange world of reflections and tricks of circumstance between the worlds of history and legend in those times.

Another family closely in the background were the Counts of Flanders, who had sent pilgrims to the Holy Land for four generations, and one of whom, Philip of Alsace, reputedly gave Chrétien de Troyes the manuscript from which he garnered the Story of the Grail.

Crudely exploited, much of this kind of material may legitimately be regarded as "glamour". Correctly understood, these mythopoeic elements that surround certain figures and events in history, giving them an archetypal resonance, are the working material of the Mysteries.

The difference between the two needs to be carefully evaluated, for much the same also occurs in fiction of a symbolic or esoteric nature - not least in the novels of Dion Fortune. In the later novels, as in the *Arthurian Formula,* we find an Atlantean strand, and statements and assumptions are sometimes made as to sexual psychology and morals that may need some qualification. We should therefore think it possible that powerful Atlantean contacts may not always have all the answers to 20th century living that they may think they possess. Although on the other hand they may be bearers of important forgotten or neglected truths that need consideration for healing the ills of current society.

All this goes to show that the prime virtues of any Mystery tradition are the exercise of Discretion and Discrimination. While we may smile condescendingly on those who seek certainty in belief in an infallible Pope, or cluck our tongues at fundamentalists who seek certainty in an infallible Book, we should beware the beam in our own eye that may assume infallibility in esoteric teacher, tradition or script. We have, on the esoteric quest, to consider all things, and seeking the still small voice of the spirit, hold fast to that which is good.

That said, over the space of the forty years I have known it, I have found the *Arthurian Formula* to be a constant challenge and stimulus that has led me by many fascinating ways in service to others and fulfilment for myself. As with that other important text in our tradition, *The Cosmic Doctrine,* its purpose is to train the mind as much as to inform it. So regarded, it can open doors in the mind that "will not again be shut", and rekindle a lamp within the soul "that has for too long been extinguished".

3
THE MASTER OF MEDICINE

One of the most exciting literary finds in the archives of the Society of the Inner Light has been a bunch of files labelled *Esoteric Therapeutics*. It had been assumed to be work of a former member, a qualified doctor of medicine, who saw long service in the Society from 1946 into the 1960's and possibly later, but who is now deceased.

However, on studying the contents in detail, it was plainly written up from records of the mediumship of Dion Fortune, with a particular contact known as the Master of Medicine, some of it going back as far as 1921.

The original intention of the communicator had been to write a book, and even to found a school of esoteric medicine, but for one reason and another the book was never published, the school never founded, although some of the teaching was privately circulated to suitably qualified individuals, and there was at one time a kind of health retreat owned by the Society at St. Albans, which may have had some connection with this initiative.

Apart from any intrinsic value the text may have in the province of the healing arts, it is of considerable interest for the light it throws upon the life and work of Dion Fortune. We find a medical and psychotherapeutic background to many stages of her life and so it is hardly surprising to find her concerned over a long period of time with a work on the subject of healing.

Her parents had been concerned in the running of a hydrotherapeutic centre. When still in her early twenties she developed an interest in psycho-analysis, and practised as a lay analyst, working at a medico-psychological clinic. She also gave public lectures on psychology which were later collected and published as *The Machinery of the Mind* with a sympathetic foreword by a well known scientist, A.G.Tansley F.R.S.

It was from this background that she gradually moved towards more fully committed esoteric interests, and the series of stories she wrote for the *Royal Magazine* in the early 1920's, *The Secrets of Dr. Taverner*, had as their protagonist an occultly informed medical practitioner.

The role model for Dr. Taverner is generally conceded to be, from her own admission, a charismatic occult teacher under whom she studied, Dr. Theodore Moriarty. It should be said he was not a medical practitioner, nor did he ever run a private nursing home. Thus he served in the main as a character sketch for her hero.

Some of the ideas in the fictional case book may well have come from another close source, a family friend and her immediate teacher in the Hermetic Order of the Golden Dawn, Maiya Curtis-Webb (later Tranchell-Hayes). She had been wedded to a distinguished psychiatrist, who was the head of a large mental hospital. It seems likely that speculative discussion between the two ladies about some of the inmates and their symptoms may well have been worked up into Dr. Taverner stories, for Dion Fortune claims that they are based on fact.

Another strong medical link was made in 1925 when Dion Fortune had a medical doctor and his sister, a nurse, as lodgers at her London headquarters, a relationship which blossomed, and in 1927 she and Dr. Thomas Penry Evans were married. Most of the contacts with the Master of Medicine in the early days are made with Dr. Evans as the principal sitter involved.

However, the first contact was recorded some time before he appeared on the scene, when as part of her psychological and esoteric researches Dion Fortune had begun to investigate the phenomena of trance. Characteristically, she did this in the most direct way possible, by attempting to do it herself. It is not to be found on the regular curriculum of the Hermetic Order of the Golden Dawn, which she had joined in 1919, but it is likely that she had been encouraged to think along these lines through her contact with Theodore Moriarty possibly from as early as 1916.

In the earliest session to have survived on record, on 11th January 1921, in the presence of Maiya Curtis-Webb, with an unknown scribe, we find a quantity of medically related communication suddenly coming through. There is no named identity recorded for the inner source of the communication, which is somewhat disjointed and even garbled. Indeed, it might be said to be apprentice work on the part of both medium and communicator – although the transcription skills of the scribe, who is unlikely to have had shorthand skills, is another debatable factor.

The communication seems to start in full spate, and goes on apparently somewhat breathlessly about the possible effect of the ductless glands (the endocrine system) in dementia praecox (now generally known as schizophrenia) and how hypnotic suggestion might be used in relation to both.

The general theme is that the emotions, or the lower astral plane, can be the cause of physical disease by acting through the etheric vehicle. The importance of the seven planes is also stressed, and their influence one upon the other, from spiritual through to the physical level.

This seems part of a series of more or less fortnightly meetings during the early part of 1921. The subject matter veers off onto more general occult themes but returns to medical topics on 15th March. Emphasis is laid on the need to distinguish between two major types of disease. On the one hand those that are genuinely physical in origins, and which act from below upwards; and on the other hand those which have an inner causation, and act from above to below in terms of the planes.

That is all we hear from this source for another six years, at any rate from what has survived on record. During this time Dion Fortune developed her mediumistic ability to the point of producing two book length manuscripts: *The Cosmic Doctrine* and the gist of *The Esoteric Philosophy of Love and Marriage*. Apart from these set pieces she also developed some inner contacts of a high and unusual quality who, in one way and another, helped and guided her in her esoteric work for the rest of her life.

One of these, generally known as David Carstairs, who claimed to have been killed at Ypres in the recent war, acted as a general introductor to most of the others, and was what in Spiritualist circles would probably be called a "guide" or "control".

Towards the beginning of August 1927, a few months after Dion Fortune and Dr. Evans were married, Carstairs came through with an announcement: "You are about to meet a teacher whom I believe has spoken to you once before, but who will come to you more frequently in the future."

Without further ado this other contact came in, announcing that he would address them on the occult side of physiology, pathology and therapeutics of mind and body; but that this knowledge, although transcending the orthodox canon, would find its place in the structure of rational science.

Accordingly, on 9th August 1927, a book began to be dictated. Its title was *The Principles of Esoteric Medicine,* and by the end of the month three chapters were complete: on the method of approach; an analysis of the causes of disease; and the anatomy of the subtle bodies.

The dictated work was interspersed with sessions of question and answer between Dr. Evans and the communicator, about whose identity there was naturally a considerable amount of speculation.

The great Renaissance occultist physician Paracelus (1493-1541) was a popular supposition, but Carstairs intervened in his inimitable style, and advised caution on any public claims as to identity. He suggested using the title "the Master of Medicine". Being Carstairs, he could not resist putting in a few supplementary hints of his own. This is what he had to say just after the sessions had begun on a regular basis:

"Hello. Seems to have settled down to his job quite happily. Decided to take you on. So you have been looking him up in *Who's Who!* He was a big Greek initiate, and he brought through what he knew, and the consequences you know. He came back again later on, and that is the incarnation you haven't traced; his last time. He has been back since the middle ages one, not so long ago either. That is his secret anyway. Hahnemann *(1755-1843 - the founder of homeopathy)* learned his ideas from him. But it doesn't matter who he is, the question is what he gives. If you are satisfied with that, all right. I should recommend that for all practical purposes you call him Master of Medicine. Avoid names, too many Shakespeares and Platos about. Never brag about your rich relations – only gets you disliked."

At the same time he made one or two important points about the problems and quality of mediumship in general:

"When you claim to contact the great minds of antiquity it is like putting a two inch pipe into a big lake, you are limited by the capacity of your medium. You are fortunate in that you have got a large bore pipe, and get quite a lot through it. But you will never get the whole through any medium, for if she were a lake she would not be a medium. If you had a pipe the same bore as the cistern, it wouldn't be a pipe."

He then went to give one or two concealed hints as to the communicator's most recent incarnation:

"No reason why you shouldn't trace it if you can. If you can catch him you have got him. I gave you hints - `bugs`. He was the father of modern drugs but he was the father of more than that, and the mother of bacteriology, but he miscarried, or to be more strictly accurate he was aborted by his professional brethren. (I use the word `bugs` in its drawing room sense.)"

A week or two later however, Carstairs refers to him directly by name - as "old Semmelweiss". This identification is very much in line with the series of concealed hints in the words we have quoted above, notably "mother," "miscarried" and "aborted", for Ignaz Semmelweis, (1818-65), one of the pioneers of bacteriology, made his name from success in maternity wards. He showed how puerperal or childbed fever, which killed a large percentage of hospitalised patients, could be virtually wiped out if doctors washed their hands in chlorine solution. This was in the days before Pasteur and Lister, and microscope technology, which eventually allowed the scientific investigation of microbes – or what Carstairs calls 'bugs'.

There seems a problem with Carstairs' assertion that Semmmelweis influenced Hahnemann, in that he only graduated the year after Hahnemann died. However, this is clarified later.

Despite this detailed information as to identity Carstairs again cautions them about being too eager to pin down contacts to specific incarnations.

"Don't be in a hurry to identify your contacts. They are apt to be rather shy birds till they get to know you better. But I will tell you who the last one was if you like to know. He was the one you thought, (i.e. Paracelsus) but that was not his last incarnation. His last will give you a clue to his psychology. I don't know how he pronounces his name. It begins with an S – Semmelweiss. That is the nearest I can get to it. He was an Austrian. *(Actually he was born Hungarian, but he qualified, and for the most part practised, and died, in Austria.)* He had a pretty tough time of it and it didn't do his temper any good. He does not suffer fools gladly, and that was one of his troubles."

In response to some direct questions about his identity, the Master of Medicine declined to be specific, but afforded some statements which support Carstairs' identification.

"I do not see that you need very greatly concern yourselves who I was or what I was. It is sufficient for you that I am willing to teach, and know what I am talking about. However, since you have framed certain questions and seem perplexed I will endeavour to clear matters up.

"With regard to the teaching used in some of my works, let me say that I wrote for my age, and I wrote in cipher, and the outward form of the cipher was in the language that the populace were accustomed to associate with learning. I wrote with my tongue in my cheek, but I got my results, and my pupils knew what I meant; but if you will translate terms of matter into terms of consciousness you also will get what I mean. You understand? If I had spoken of consciousness and the faculties of the soul, I should have been trespassing upon holy ground. It was enough that I should estrange my professional brethren, without transgressing the rules of Holy Church into the bargain. *(This seems to support the Paracelus identification, along with an interesting hint upon the way to approach Paracelsus' obscure, alchemically loaded, written texts.)*

"I have had certain work to do in medicine, I took my initiation in Greece, and it was an initiation of the way of healing; and before that I had been one of the Therapeutoi of Egypt. On my initiation in Greece I won my freedom, but I elected to return. I returned twice. I wanted to put through certain tasks in relation to medicine. In each case my success was partial; the reason being that my initiations were imperfect and incomplete. I have justly been called the Father of Modern Drug Systems.

"There are two main systems, as you know. Of one I myself laid the foundations personally. The other was founded by my favourite pupil – reincarnating for the purpose; and I assisted him, as I am assisting you. *(This would clear up our little time problem, mentioned above, if he inspired Hahnemann from the inner planes, before reincarnating himself.)*

"I never intended to reincarnate again, therefore I sought to work through my pupil; but I had to reincarnate again, because I had the science of medicine in my care. It might be said that I was its patron saint, though I had but little claim to saintliness. I reincarnated again in order to try and deal with surgical sepsis, and I failed, because I came too soon. I came before the high powered microscope, and therefore I could not demonstrate my discoveries. It remained for another man *(probably Lister 1827-1912)* to do that work, but it has been done, and that is all that matters.

"You will never see again what I have seen, when from one ward we were losing eighty percent of normal confinements. We had to close the wards, it was all we could do. I have seen hospitals pulled down because the mortality was such they dare not continue them. They were known as `Pest-hausen` in my time. They were well named. *(A double play on words – he refers to the Maternity Clinic at Pest, a town which is now part of Budapest.)*

"I have been the father of the modern system of drugs. I was the forerunner of modern asepsis. I desire to be for the third and last time a pioneer in medicine. After that, I shall take my freedom and go on."

"The work I have in mind this time concerns the inter-relation of mind and body, the mental factor in disease, and the mental factor in therapeutics."

In confiding this high purpose he goes on to give some heartfelt advice.

"Now my friends, and brother of my profession, I have made mistakes before in my work, and I do not want to make them again. I made them in that chief incarnation, of which you know, by estranging my professional brethren through what was really my bad manners and unpardonable conduct. I despised them, and I let them see it, which is fatal; and in my last incarnation I made the mistake again of estranging my brethren by alleging what I could not prove. I was right, and they know it now, but I had not got what Lister had – Pasteur's work, and the high powered magnification. I knew, but I could not prove. You will know, if you listen to me, a good many things which you will not be able to prove. Learn by my experience. A still tongue, my friend, saves many a broken head and a broken heart. If you desire to give a strong tonic, you give it in measured doses; but I took my patient, the medical profession, by the nose, and forced the bottle between its teeth, and poured down the dose, and my patient had convulsions."

"The measured dose for new teaching, my friend. Too much medicine can be poisonous, and so can too much truth."

Indeed the Master of Medicine developed a somewhat acerbic reputation, being described at one point by David Carstairs as a "very raspy old gentleman... ... ... not in the best of tempers this evening." This was on an occasion when he had been pressed by some of those present upon the ethics of the use of animals in medical research. This he declined to condemn outright, but qualified his attitude by saying: "As a matter of fact, in the researches of esoteric medicine, animal experimentation will be of very little use to you, because in human beings the mental factor is a very large one and falsifies many of the results. But you must remember this, that all your esoteric medicine which concerns the boundary line of mind and body can have no other basis than a sound knowledge of anatomy and physiology. ... ... I do not suggest that as individuals it is incumbent upon you to take up this line of research work, but I would counsel you not to decry the work of those upon whose results you must base your own researches."

He continued with some very straight talking, telling them that "the world is not made according to the pattern of a pink sugar heaven," and that they must learn to distinguish between compassion and sentimentality.

A contact who had been responsible for passing through *The Cosmic Doctrine* here intervened by way of mediation to those who plainly felt some sense of outrage: "The Master of Medicine did not tell you that you were to be deliberately cruel. But he did tell you that you must face facts – and that is what we all tell you – you cannot evade facts... ... ... You may say 'these things are deplorable, is there anything that can be done?' But you cannot say they are not so, and that is why we train you; because the tendency of the spiritually-minded is to be nice-minded; we want you to be true-minded. There is a distinction."

This suggests that not all who were admitted to this early work were up to a standard that would be expected nowadays. This is never more apparent than in an interview recorded between the Master of Medicine and an aspirant to who sought to offer her services for the healing ministry without having given too much analytical thought as to her abilities.

She was given some forewarning in a preliminary interview with the Master who was Dion Fortune's principle contact: "You must remember, in dealing with him, that he is a man who, in his last incarnation, which of course is the personality in which he manifests, was accustomed to deal with medical students a hundred years ago... ... ... A man of noble soul, and vast intellect; and you must strive to see the compassionate heart behind the rough tongue. It is because he was a man of extreme sensitiveness of nature that he covered himself with a thorny covering."

The interview, thorns and all, proceeded as follows:

M. of M.: Greeting, what is it I can do for you?

Dr. Evans: Our sister wishes to bring her gifts to the altar, and thinks that she has a special gift of healing.

M. of M.: Well, my daughter, now what about this special gift of healing? What makes you think you have got a special gift of healing?

Querant: Because I have used it. I have been told I have it.

M. of M.: And you have used it and got results? How long have you been using it?

Querant: For a year.

M. of M.: How many cases have you had?

Querant: Only three, but one continued for eight months.

M. of M.:	It isn't the length of time, it is the results you have got. It is no especial virtue to have a case a long time, rather the other way about. Now of your three, in how many cases was the original diagnosis confirmed? In how many were they discharged cured? In how many were they improved? In how many was there no change? And how many were killed? It is no good coming to me and saying I have got this case cured. What you want is the necessary statistics. That is the test.
Querant:	I have not given the treatment.
M. of M.:	That is rather peculiar – yet you have had three cases. How many have you cured?
Querant:	Two, and the third was a faith cure.
M. of M.:	It does not matter what, if you cured the case. Perhaps it was due to lack of faith. But it does not matter what you call it – if you cure by faith or jalop, I don't mind, if you have a cure. Two out of three – that is a presentable proportion.
Querant:	The one I had for eight months was a different thing.
M. of M.:	There is as much skill in managing the patient as in treating the human body. You cannot put a patient in a strait waistcoat. One does not treat the disease and forget the patient; and

that is where experience comes in, and the art of handling human nature, which is as much part of the art of medicine as the technical aspects. A man may know his science side, but unless he can handle human nature he is not going to succeed in practice. Well now, what do you want to do?

Querant: Can I be trained?

M. of M.: You can be trained, certainly. I cannot make anything of you till you are trained, that is quite certain. And I will give you a word of warning – healing is not a simple thing. So my advice to you is this – learn the technique of the thing you want to do. And remember this – never start your treatment till you are sure of your diagnosis, otherwise you are no better off than the vendor of patent medicines. Now what do you understand by spiritual healing? Come along. Don`t crib.

Querant: I was told... ... ...

M. of M.: Don`t tell me what you were told. What do you mean by spiritual healing?

Querant: Laying on of hands.

M. of M.: I call that massage. What have the hands to do with it? Think it out.

Querant: Being a channel to flow through.

M. of M.:	What is the spiritual force?
Querant:	The Christ force.
M. of M.:	Of what kind is that?
Querant:	The gift of healing.
M. of M.:	Now we are back where we started.
Querant:	I want to learn.
M. of M.:	Clarity of ideas is the beginning of wisdom. So unless you begin to think more clearly, I cannot teach you. Now what do you mean when you say spiritual healing? You have got a label, but you don`t know what it is tied to. What do you mean by healing?
Querant:	Take a case of hernia – by laying on of hands I have reduced the hernia.
M. of M.:	How do you know it was a hernia?
Querant:	It was diagnosed.
M. of M.:	How do you know you reduced it?
Querant:	By examination.
M. of M.:	And how did you heal it?
Querant:	By putting my hands on it.

M. of M.:	You see, my daughter, if you want to function with spiritual healing, and don't know what spirit is, and what healing is, you are not a safe guide. What happens when you do this? Shall I tell you? You are going into a medical hospital, into the dispensary in the dark, and you are taking down the first bottle you lay your hands on, and you are pouring some into a glass and handing it to the patient. Now there is a glyph for you to meditate on. One of these days you will be giving the wrong bottle.
Querant:	But I am not doing it.
M. of M.:	That is a relief to my mind. Now spiritual healing is a very important thing. I will tell you what it is, since you can't tell me. "Healing" means making the abnormal normal; bringing that which has got out of line into line. And "Spirit" is the parent essence of life – life before it takes on form. Spiritual healing means straightening things out, beginning at the top, and that force has to be translated down the planes; and on each plane it functions according to the nature of that plane. In spiritual things it functions spiritually. In mental things it functions mentally. In astral things it functions astrally. And in physical things it functions materially. And what you need to learn is, to know at what point in the planes lesion has occurred, and pick it up there. And if the lesion is on the spiritual plane, nothing but spiritual

healing will touch it, and no surgeon or physician can do anything for it. If on the mental plane, you must express your healing in terms of psychology. If on the astral, you will express it in terms of magic; and if on the physical plane, you will express it in terms of surgery and medicine. And what you need to know is, how to place your case; otherwise, my daughter, you are going to burn your fingers. So that is what you need to know if you do spiritual healing.

Querant: I have no intention of treating anyone unless I am trained.

M. of M.: That is sound policy. Mind you stick to it. You probably won't. That is why we say spiritual healing is not nearly so simple as it looks, and the trouble comes when you get hold of the wrong type of case. And that is where the technical knowledge comes in – in sorting out the cases. But I will say this – there is no case in the world that would not be the better for spiritual healing. But there are only a small percentage of cases where spiritual healing is going to cure by itself. It is part of a much larger whole. You are playing one instrument in a quartet, and you will make some very funny noises if you play by yourself. And the true therapy contains all the elements I have mentioned – spiritual, psychological, magical and physical; and in every case they are present in different proportions, for everything that happens on one plane reflects down the planes always. And therefore, my daughter, the spiritual healer plays a part in the orchestra — not a solo. And what you need to understand is the technique of what you are doing. See what you are doing. Why you do it. How you do it. When to do it, and still more important, when not to do it. Of the non-physical healings there are several types. Spiritual healing is only one. There is also psychological healing; and magical work; and etheric healing. So there are four distinct types. Now, my daughter, I have told you something of what it means; and I have tried to make you think. If I have succeeded in making you see that it is not as simple as it looks, I have done you considerable service. Now is there anything else, or have you had enough?

Querant: I thank you for all you have said. I will think it over, because I wish to serve the Masters, and that is all I think I have got to offer. Perhaps I can serve in some other way.

M. of M.: That is more sensible. It is more to the point to do what is wanted, than what you want to do.

It is about this time that the plans in store for Dion Fortune and her group began to be formulated in some detail by those upon the inner planes. That is to say, the major Fraternity that was about to be formed from what had been up to then little more than a small circle of friends. Carstairs gives due warning of this in an short snatch of conversation with Thomas Penry Evans.

Carstairs: Now, do you see what these chaps are driving at?

Dr. Evans: To establish a school on the basis of discipline.

Carstairs: And they don't want molly-coddles. If you can't stand a hammering, go home, see? ... ... It is not a bit of use pretending it is a bed of roses; it isn't. There is a great deal of difference between half-ideals and true ideals. That is what they are hammering into you. No one had more ideals than old Semmelweis, and no one was so true to his ideals. But we are not out for those short cuts to comfort. We are out for something bigger than that. You can't say where it begins or ends. But they will teach you to handle elemental forces. That is why they are banging away at you. Take the rough with the smooth, it is no good being squeamish in this line of work.

1928 seems to have been a crucial year so far as the work of the group was concerned. It saw the start of publication of the *Inner Light Magazine* and public announcement of the foundation of the Community of the Inner Light, a forerunner of the Fraternity and Society. This seems, of necessity, to have pushed work with the Master of Medicine somewhat to one side. Therefore we find, on 26th May 1928, a somewhat plaintive remark from him to Dr. Evans: "I shall be very glad indeed when this matter can go forward. No doubt you will also. The delay is annoying to both of us. Can you see your way at your end?" To which Dr. Evans replies: "Not quite clearly yet, sir."

This seems to refer to the setting up of some kind of school or clinic in a place set apart, for the Master of Medicine goes on to say: "It is not possible to do our form of therapeutic work, except in a place in which we can make our mental atmosphere. Just as the surgeon must have his conditions, so must the psychologist."

Later in the year a conversation is recorded between Dion Fortune's principal contact and Dr. Evans and C.T.Loveday, discussing immediate priorities for the work ahead. Mr. Loveday is hoping to find more time to devote to the Christian Mystic Lodge and further instruction on *The Cosmic Doctrine,* whilst Dr. Evans seeks regular meetings for instruction by the Master of Medicine. To these representations they receive the somewhat two-edged response that they will get what they invoke for.

Meetings between the Master of Medicine and Dr. Evans are recorded throughout the next five years, although it is surprising how few and far between they seem to be. There are only six meetings recorded during the whole period from 1928 to 1932, resulting in just 24 pages of typescript, no more than had been received in the cluster of initial meetings in August 1927. It is possible however that the record of trance transcripts is incomplete.

We do not find any further verbatim records until 1941. During this time much water had flowed under the bridge for Dr. Evans and Dion Fortune, including the break up of their marriage. Personal details and precise dates are lacking but we know that Dr. Evans went to advise the Republican government on child nutrition in the Spanish Civil War, and although he was chased out of Barcelona by Franco's forces in 1938, it seems he did not return to Dion Fortune or to the Society. He later remarried, after Dion Fortune's death, and died in 1959, a well liked and much respected member of the medical community in Amersham, Buckinghamshire.

During the war years Dion Fortune tried to continue work with the Master of Medicine, and to make up for the absence of her husband invited other medically qualified doctors in his stead. As they were not members of her Fraternity, nor familiar with its assumptions, beliefs and culture, this met with somewhat mixed results.

A transcript of May 18th 1941, shows the invited doctor deliberately testing the medical knowledge of the trance contact with questions such as: "Can you tell me the treatment for high blood pressure?" and "What is the best way of treating a burn?"

The somewhat surprising reply from the inner plane communicator, in the light of all that has gone before, is: "I myself am not a doctor so could perhaps not help very much in that matter."

A closer examination of the text, however, throws some interesting light on the mechanisms of trance and the supposed identity of contacts. Thus, he goes on to say: "There are others with more knowledge but at the present moment communication is not established. But I could help you on questions of general principles." In other words, the current communicator would seem to be a go-between of some kind, rather than the original Master of Medicine.

Following this less than promising start the course of the interview was led onto more general topics by the occultists present, W.K.Creasy, a senior member of the Fraternity at the time, and Mrs Tranchell-Hayes, who turns up here again at Dion Fortune's side, for the first time apparently since the early experiments of twenty years before.

The doctor concerned in this first interview was not asked back, but a rather more productive series of interviews followed with a doctor of less sceptical turn of mind. A consequence of the more relaxed atmosphere is that it leads on to a more specialist series of exchanges, including some quite detailed clinical discussion with respect to actual cases, for instance of infantile paralysis (nowadays known as poliomyelitis.)

At one point the communicator draws attention to this phenomenon of quality of communication, saying: "You understand, do you not, that I am picking up the data from your mind and interpreting it from my viewpoint? .... As I say, I am not a doctor and you are, and I deal with abstract ideas, and I can, as it were, read these from your mind and make use of them in talking to you. If I were discussing with a layman I should not have them to make use of. That is why I have to teach Esoteric Medicine to one who can supply me with the raw materials. But I deal with abstractions on my plane of consciousness, and you deal with dense matter on your plane of consciousness, and we meet halfway, and I link up my concepts with yours and so make what is abstract concrete, so that you can make the application."

This suggests that the presence of Dr. Penry Evans had been an important factor in the earlier communications. It also raises a point in regard to the mechanics of trance communication that the quality of the sitters is also an important factor.

There is also evidence that sometimes there may be another communicator behind the assumed or usual identity of a contact. Thus on one occasion, following some detailed discussion, the communicator says "We have been honoured tonight. We have been fortunate enough to have the presence of one who does not very often communicate. He can give you what I cannot. You no doubt noticed the point at which the change took place. He is not a very ready communicator."

These concerns with the technicalities of trance are dealt with in more detail in *Spiritualism and Occultism,* a much expanded version of Dion Fortune's original *Spiritualism in the Light of Occult Science* (Thoth Publications 1999). It is true that trance mediumship as a means of communication has been phased out in recent years in favour of a more conscious mode of mentation that is called "mediation". However experience suggests that much the same questions of contact identity remain, whether or not the channel for the communications be in a conscious or unconscious state at the time.

Dion Fortune's meetings with doctors lasted until the end of 1941 when the communicator expressed a preference for dictating lectures rather than having clinical conversations. At much the same time a set of confidential papers began to be circulated to selected recipients, entitled *Esoteric Therapeutics* and described as "Teaching received from the Inner Planes by the Fraternity of the Inner Light".

Later, at some time after the war, all the material along these lines was gathered up and collated into reasonable order and privately run off under the title of *Esoteric Medicine,* probably under the supervision of the qualified medical doctor whose name was upon one of the files of this material.

To a layman it contains a fascinating run down of elements of more general occult interest than the specialist vocation of healing. There are sections for example on the chakras or etheric centres and also on means of developing clairvoyance and intuitive powers in the matter of spiritual, psychological and physical diagnosis.

Some care needs to be exercised in its general publication insofar that much of the information is up to seventy years old, and apart from any possible controversy over esoteric aspects of medicine, some of the medical terms that were used have now radically changed – some of which we have drawn attention to within the body of this article.

Nonetheless there seems to be much of value within the material that deserves to see the light of day, whether or not it lives up to the high expectations of the Master of Medicine when he began to deliver it has now been published under the title of *Principles of Esoteric Healing* (Sun Chalice, 2000).

4
DION FORTUNE AND THE TRIUMPH OF THE MOON

The Triumph of the Moon, subtitled *A History of Modern Pagan Witchcraft,* (Oxford University Press, 1999) written by Ronald Hutton, Professor of History at the University of Bristol, shows every sign of being an important milestone in the study of contemporary religious thought and belief.

It is a natural development from Professor Hutton's previous work *The Stations of the Sun* (O.U.P. 1996), a highly readable and comprehensive history of the ritual year in Britain, both Christian and pagan, which in turn developed from two more specialist works, *The Pagan Religions of the Ancient British Isles* and *The Rise and Fall of Merry England.* The first of these was a survey of religious beliefs in the British Isles from the Old Stone Age through Celtic and Romano-British paganism to the survival of pre-Christian beliefs and imagery in the Middle Ages. As if a coverage from 10,000 B.C. to 1000 A.D. were not enough it concluded with some thoughts about the stirrings of a modern pagan revival. The second, considerably more focussed in time, was a study of the ritual year in medieval England and Wales between 1400 and 1700.

It is not our intention to review any of these books at length, save to say that they deserve a place on any serious occultist's bookshelf. Our remarks concern how Dion Fortune appears to their author.

She features quite prominently in Chapter 10 of *The Triumph of the Moon* as one of four modern figures, active between 1900 and 1950, who Professor Hutton considers "had a direct and obvious influence upon modern pagan witchcraft and have been acknowledged by many modern witches as sources of inspiration."

These four figures are Aleister Crowley (1875-1947), Dion Fortune (1890-1946), Robert Graves (1895-1985) and Dr. Margaret Murray (1862-1963), author of *The Witch Cult in Western Europe* (1921) and *The God of the Witches* (1933). By virtue of certain elements of their work they are described as god-parents (or perhaps more accurately "goddess-parents") of what Professor Hutton recognises to be a new religion – modern pagan witchcraft.

Dion Fortune was also briefly mentioned in *The Pagan Religions in the British Isles* in the context of beliefs surrounding Glastonbury Tor:

"…in the 1930`s, the mystic Violet Firth (Dion Fortune) had a vision of a processional way around the Tor, constructed and used by refugees from Atlantis. Her idea was taken up in 1969, when Glastonbury was filling with people seeking the arcane and the supernatural, by Geoffrey Russell. He suggested that the terraces were a sacred way of the Neolithic or early Bronze Age, and mapped out the presumed route, winding up the hill in a flattened spiral. As a result, modern pagans and earth mystics can have the immense satisfaction of following this path in the belief that they are participating in a genuine ancient ritual."

To archaeologists, the terraces on Glastonbury Tor have always been presumed to be typical medieval or iron age hillside field systems and in the light of such research as has been done they have not been particularly ready to change their opinions. Whether or not they should ultimately prove to be right or wrong the important point at issue here is how powerfully a mystic's vision can affect our beliefs about the ancient world. In this respect Dion Fortune played a role as a modern myth maker whatever the assumptions of archaeology.

Important questions are raised here for those of the neo-pagan movement who, encouraged by Margaret Murray, assume their faith to be a very ancient one that has survived intact and unbroken through the middle ages until its revival in modern times. Breaking the news in the nicest possible way, Professor Hutton points out that despite considerable research there is very little evidence for such a belief. In short, although neo-paganism may have certain resonances with ancient belief and practice, there is no unbroken line throughout the ages, and such can be no more than a wishful modern reconstruction and interpretation.

A modern occultist is unlikely to have any great problems with this, but to a number of neo-pagans, who approach their beliefs in the nature of a religion rather than as part of a magical philosophy, the shock may be rather like that experienced by a fundamentalist Christian when confronted with the results of modern Bible criticism.

However, history is a treacherous subject, as every historian knows. Even complete and accurate evidence from the past, (if this is ever possible), can tell only part of the story, and much depends upon the interpretation of its significance by the individual historian. It has even been suggested that true history is an impossible dream, for all is in the eye of a beholder. Thus a history of the human race penned by a socialist humanist, H.G.Wells, in *A Short History of the World* presents a very different picture from that of one written by a Christian apologist such as G.K.Chesterton in *The Everlasting Man.*

On a rather less comprehensive scale we find much the same kind of problems coming into focus when we examine the life and work of Dion Fortune, particularly as it relates to the pagan movement. Professor Hutton's general view of her is as "a leader in the world of early twentieth-century British occultism. Indeed because of her writings she is now its foremost female figure." Nonetheless, some of his detailed remarks seem to me to be somewhat wide of the mark.

In comparing her with fellow occultist Aleister Crowley, he sees the main difference, not in terms of moral calibre as might seem the more obvious, but in the light of education. Crowley, with the benefit of a public school and Cambridge education, supplemented by extensive travel, never had any time for the myth of Atlantis; whereas Dion Fortune who, like most women of her time, had no university education, in her ignorance knew no better than to accept the myth of Atlantis as literal truth. I have to find this plausible but somewhat patronising assumption unsatisfactory on no less than three counts.

First, an acceptance or rejection of the Atlantis myth is not necessarily a matter of education. It plays a major part in the philosophy of Rudolf Steiner, for example, who was bright enough to have been appointed editor of the scientific works of Goethe. By extension one will have to include other anthroposophically and theosophically persuaded characters who demonstrate formidable intellects and educational qualifications, whilst to my observation there seems to be no obvious correlation in esoteric circles between those who reject Atlantis out of hand and those who have progressed beyond their A levels.

Secondly, the matter of Atlantis was not entirely discredited by scientific thought in the 1920's, when Dion Fortune wrote upon these matters. For instance Lieutenant Colonel Fawcett's ill fated expedition into the Brazilian jungle in 1925 was backed by responsible learned bodies such as the Royal Geographical Society and the American Geographical Society. To quote the Daily Express of August 21st 1928:

"He had already gone far towards proving his contention that there existed in this region a majestic civilisation perhaps 10,000 years old, ante-dating Egypt; that it held the secret of a mysterious light, possibly based on knowledge of basic atomic force; that this ancient people were familiar with astronomy, and that they had perhaps the oldest highly developed indigenous culture in the history of the world. He had so far analysed and articulated the findings of his previous expeditions that he was ready to announce his conclusions and risk his scientific reputation on them."

This may not seem quite the same idea as a submerged Atlantic continent but in Fawcett's mind it was very much connected with Atlantis, as he states categorically in a letter of 9th November 1924 to Margaret Lumley Brown:

"There is a Community, which is a relic of Atlantean civilization and preserves complete records of it ... Their whereabouts is not known to geographers, nor are they very numerous. I happen to be an explorer myself, of the pioneer genus, and the discovery was the fruit of patient research and no little suffering and risk. The value of the discovery is simply incalculable, as the mere proof of an Atlantean civilization, with an alphabetical script and a scientific knowledge in some ways ahead of ours, would revolutionize both Science and Religion."

Margaret Lumley Brown, a cultured woman of considerable clairvoyant gifts, had written to Fawcett as the result of some psychic experiences she had had that seemed connected with Atlantis. More detail on this will can be found in *Pythoness* (Sun Chalice, 2000) which contains her story and extracts from this correspondence. She too, perhaps more so than Dion Fortune, compiled a dossier of visions that she had had that apparently related to an ancient doomed continent that she was willing to call Atlantis.

This brings us to our third point. When it comes to practical occultism we have to be very careful as to what we impute to be "literal" truth. As Dion Fortune has said on more than one occasion, it is necessary to believe implicitly in what one is doing at the time if the magic is going to work. Analysis and intellectual speculation come afterward. This can be the cause of some misunderstanding when occultist talks to academic, and particularly so as occultists themselves, in the general run of things, are less meticulous than they might be in differentiating, even in their own minds, between the literally true and what is mythopoeically so.

Atlantis aside, Professor Hutton likes to think of Dion Fortune in terms of being a devout mystical Christian, albeit a very unorthodox one, during the period 1914 to 1930. He then sees her, after a period of silent reassessment, undergoing a kind of pagan enlightenment in about 1935 as a result of the influence of three men, D.H.Lawrence, Thomas Penry Evans and Charles Seymour. This may be a perspective favoured by neo-pagans who would like to see Dion Fortune as one entirely won over to their cause, after a blighted start in life, but it hardly concurs with the facts. However, it may well be a common misconception, for it is one assumed by Professor Hutton on the basis of published work available to him in volume form. This however does not appear to include issues of the *Inner Light Magazine* from 1927 through to 1940 or her Weekly and Monthly Letters circulated to students and associates after that date — to say nothing of her private archive. From these it is plain that she ever pursued a broader three-fold way. However, to return to Professor Hutton's thesis, let us take a closer look at his three influential men.

Any influence from Lawrence was a purely literary one and there is no suggestion that they ever met or corresponded. She almost certainly read him with enthusiasm, and (probably unconsciously) named one of her heroines, Ursula Brangwyn in *The Winged Bull,* from a character in *The Rainbow.* One would expect a certain enthusiasm for Lawrence in his advocacy of sexual liberation, for Dion Fortune was no prude by the standards of her day.

It is easy to make early works such as *The Esoteric Philosophy of Love and Marriage* or *The Problem of Purity* a butt for hilarity, without taking account of the climate of the times in which she wrote.

The Problem of Purity, for example, although not published until 1927, dates in essence from before 1916 when she was a trainee at the Medico-Psychological Institute. She may have liked to pass herself off in later life as a pioneer psychoanalyst but in reality she was a student at an experimental clinic, working under the supervision of medical personnel, having not long before recovered from a nervous breakdown of her own, as the result of a bullying employer, as described in *Psychic Self-Defence*. She was no more than a girl of 24, of sheltered up-bringing, whose previous experience in sexual matters was rearing chickens at Studley Horticultural College, now striving to cope with the depths of sexual guilt of those in need of paramedical counselling.

This was a time when young men were innocent and idealistic enough to go cheerily off to war, their girl friends presenting white feathers as a token of cowardice to those who did not. There they were soon introduced to the realities of the twentieth century as the victims of mechanised warfare. Here, in the terms of contemporary psychology, they were expected to suppress their instinct of self-preservation under fire, as at home they had been expected to suppress their instinct of reproduction, in times when sex before marriage and contraception for working class women was beyond the pale of civilised conversation.

One could hardly expect Dion Fortune in the climate of those times to have advocated the sexual freedoms that have become the commonplace of our own more liberated times. In this respect the alleged "psychic masturbation" (a sniggering epithet borrowed from Alan Richardson) in *The Problem of Purity* should be viewed in a slightly different context. It consists of visualising a jet of force, generated from the base of the spine, shooting up through the top of the head towards some worthy cause. Whether or not this should prove an effective method of sublimation for those assailed with libidinous thoughts, it seems worthy of comment for anticipating Israel Regardie's similar teaching in *The Art of True Healing* and *The Middle Pillar* of the 1930's. It is perhaps just as well that Moina MacGregor Mathers was in the last year of her life when *The Problem of Purity* was published, in remembrance of how distraught she had been at the publication of the much less specific *Esoteric Philosophy of Love and Marriage* a few years before.

If Dion Fortune's publicly expressed sexual attitudes seem dated by later standards then much the same could be said about her allegedly elitist views with regard to nations, races or classes. It may now seem self-evident that imperialism is not a "good thing" but Empire Day was still being celebrated until beyond the 2nd World War, and in many of her remarks Dion Fortune was simply speaking in the accepted language of a middle class woman of her day.

She had been genuinely distressed in 1919 when it appeared to her that an Indian occultist was set on undermining British aspirations. With the benefit of political hindsight we might well feel his sentiments to have been justified, and that the sympathies of Annie Besant, President of the Theosophical Society, towards Indian independence were commendably enlightened. This was not the issue that caused Dion Fortune to break with the Theosophical Society however, as Ronald Hutton is inclined to think.

The problem was a religious one, concerning the Star in the East movement, which from small beginnings in 1909 had largely taken over the Theosophical Movement, including the Old Catholic (renamed Liberal Catholic) church, as a means of presenting a Hindu boy, Krishnamurti, to the world as a new Messiah or World Teacher.

Dion Fortune and Thomas Loveday joined the Theosophical Society via its Christian Mystic Lodge in 1925 as a deliberate effort to oppose this movement from within. Dion Fortune became President of this Lodge and when things came to open vituperation with Bishop Piggott of the Liberal Catholic

Church, they duly resigned in 1927 and formed the Fraternity of the Inner Light. They left a caucus of like-minded sympathisers behind to continue the opposition, but in 1929 the Star in the East movement came to an end when Krishnamurti repudiated his role. As it happens he developed into a respected teacher in his own right, but without any need for hyped up Messianic aspirations.

Thomas Penry Evans, Professor Hutton's second chosen influence upon Dion Fortune, as an enthusiastic Celt, no doubt played an important role, although having met her in 1925 and married her in 1927 it is unlikely that he caused any alleged change in her attitudes from Christianity to paganism in the mid-1930's. He may well have introduced a Celtic and Elemental stream to the run of things, to the Hermetic influence inherited from Moriarty and the Golden Dawn, and the Christian bias of Charles Loveday, but the remarkable Chant of the Elements which possessed a group of them on Glastonbury Tor at Whitsun 1926 shows that the Green Ray could perfectly well work alongside the Purple Ray, to use the terminology of the time.

Professor Hutton seems not to have been aware of Dion Fortune's constant stream of writing in the *Inner Light Magazine,* which from October 1927 was a gaping maw that had to be filled month in month out until paper rationing killed it in August 1940. A number of her books first appeared serialised in its pages. Thus what he assumes to be a time of silence and reassessment before the appearance of *The Winged Bull* was on the contrary a time of intense activity.

During this period she wrote two works on Spiritualism as well as a series of articles allied to the Guild of the Master Jesus together with *Mystical Meditations on the Collects,* and between

1931 and 1934 her magnum opus *The Mystical Qabalah,* the beginnings of which were a series of visions she began to have in 1930.

She then proceeded to try to expound the more practical details of Qabalah, as she understood it, in a trilogy of novels: *The Winged Bull, The Goat-foot God,* and *The Sea Priestess* published in 1935, '36 and `38. As she states in two articles in the magazine, one of them an extended three-parter, her aim in them is a practical exegesis of Qabalistic principles, each particularly relevant to a Sephirah on the Tree of Life. Although she does not say so in so many words, these are plainly Tiphareth, Malkuth and Yesod respectively.

Charles Seymour is the third element in Ronald Hutton's trio of pagan influences on Dion Fortune. He was undoubtedly a great organisational asset to the Fraternity. A retired and very experienced army officer who had taken a Master's degree on retirement, he joined the Fraternity in 1933 and in just over a year was taking high ritual office and had also virtually taken over as Director of Studies in the role of Executive Officer of the Fraternity. He also began to contribute a long series of articles to the magazine, thus relieving Dion Fortune of some of her unremitting literary burden.

He suffered something of a set-back in the Autumn of 1936 however when a New Epoch was announced, and the Fraternity formally divided into three elements. Charles Loveday headed up the Christian side, Dion Fortune ruled the Hermetic, while the Green Ray went not to Seymour but to Tom Penry Evans. Soon after this Dion Fortune was enabled, through a generous donation from a member, to set up in the Belfry, a converted church in West Halkin Street, and to lay on public performances of her Rite of Isis, in which Seymour played a prominent part.

Hutton is on safer ground here but goes rather badly astray by asserting that in 1939 Dion Fortune's tremendous flow of literary output came to an end. This is partly because he is apparently unaware of the flow of Weekly and Monthly Letters that replaced the Inner Light magazine during the war years. Although not finding the dignity of print until comparatively recently this included *The Circuit of Force* and *Principles of Hermetic Philosophy,* also *The Esoteric Philosophy of Astrology.* Privately circulated were *Principles of Esoteric Healing* (spanning a period from 1927 to 1942) and *The Arthurian Formula,* of 1941/2 vintage.

The Circuit of Force and to a certain extent *The Principles of Hermetic Philosophy* drew much of its impetus from her association with the academic Bernard Bromage who was translating some Hindu tantrik texts. *The Principles of Esoteric Healing* dated from early work with Dr. Penry Evans whilst later work on this and the Arthurian work came from a collaboration with her old mentor Maiya Tranchell-Hayes (formerly Curtis-Webb).

However distinguished a historian may be, he can only be as good as his sources, which can become something of a liability when they are less than faultless secondary ones. Thus a contributing factor to Professor Hutton's deviation from fact is an undue reliance on Alan Richardson's works which tend to give rather too much credence to some of Christine Campbell Thompson's perceptions.

It is thus rather sad to see a grand old trouper like W.K.Creasy written off as "a mystical Christian of narrow minded piety" in a reputable academic history book on no more basis than second hand gossip in Alan Richardson's Priestess: *"It was said* that the chief rumour monger within 3 QT was William Creasy whose suspicious mind was aided by an active imagination". (The italics are mine and one wonders who the rumour monger was who said it! From evidence of archival papers, it seems rather to have been Creasy who was the victim of malignant gossip when he was working with Dion Fortune.) Furthermore, *Dancers to the Gods,* calls him "an intense and apparently narrow man ...a Christian Mysticky sort of person."

Let me say now, as one who knew him personally, that nothing could be further from the truth. He was a kindly, experienced man of the world, a retired banker, whose magical name at one stage of his esoteric career, Sandalphon of Earth, hardly fits the above caricature. Initiated into the Fraternity on the same day as Christine Campbell Thompson on 27th February 1934, he rose to be Deputy Warden, and acting Warden for a time after Dion Fortune's death. One of his last tasks was the selection of old Dion Fortune articles for inclusion in the volumes *Aspects of Occultism* and *Applied Magic* during 1961. These works, which include articles on the Worship of Isis, The Astral Plane, Non-Humans, Black Magic and A Magical Body hardly suggest a narrow minded Christian piety.

In fairness to Professor Hutton, I have no wish to cast doubt on the value of his book as a whole by concentrating my narrow range of expertise upon a small section of it. We did exchange some letters on the subject at the beginning of 1998, when his book was being prepared, and although Professor Hutton has chosen to stick with his own original perceptions he is gracious enough to acknowledge that there may be another side to things, in his concluding remarks on Dion Fortune:

"There are thus some puzzles in the story, and indeed the whole sequence of events which I have proposed above is heavily dependent upon my own perspective and the sources available to me. To a cabbalist, for example, her spate of publication in the 1930's could be quite reasonably characterized as engendered by her first really considerable work, *The Mystical Qabalah* (1935) and devoted to working out a series of ideas dependent upon the latter. Another perspective would emphasize the continual interplay in her life of three different traditions, hermetic and ritual magic, paganism, and mystical Christianity, and suggest that all that altered was the current balance of interest between them. Her apparent gaps in publication were spanned by her regular expression of views in the magazine of her order, the Inner Light, which was not available to me; although (according to those who have had access to it) they broadly reflect the shifts of interest found in her books."

Finer points of historiography aside, in the whole of the Dion Fortune story it has to be said that things would have been a great deal simpler if those who guarded her inheritance over the years (and possibly destroyed some of it) had been a little more forthcoming in giving access to interested parties in the outside world for genuine research. Those who are denied information will naturally have a tendency to fill the vacuum with guesswork and speculation.

I feel somewhat unfairly advantaged in having been given the run of the archives in recent times, and I can only hope that the resulting work, *Dion Fortune and the Inner Light* from Thoth Publications will prove worthy of the remarkable individual whose story it seeks to tell.

As Professor Hutton concludes: "she was plainly a complex thinker, whose career defies any simple formulations."

I do not think anyone can argue with that!

5
FROM WATCHERS OF AVALON
TO THE CHURCH OF THE GRAAL

In the various biographical works relating to Dion Fortune there is often scant reference to Charles Thomas Loveday, and what there is tends to be inaccurate, even bizarrely so, confusing him with one of Aleister Crowley`s acolytes.

He was in fact a most important friend, companion and colleague of hers from their first chance meeting at Glastonbury in 1922 through to the end of their lives, and from their early work together there eventually blossomed the Fraternity of the Inner Light.

He was largely responsible for finding the money to buy a plot of land at the foot of Glastonbury Tor, where they erected a number of chalets to serve as an esoteric centre for their work, and a further personal legacy provided a headquarters in a fashionable area of London. The affectionate nickname of "His Nibs" (later shortened to "Nibs") reflected his crucial role in the early years, and he remained an important force in the Fraternity when other major players such as Dr. Penry Evans, (Dion Fortune's husband) and Colonel C.R.F. Seymour ("the forgotten mage") had come and gone. Today his mortal remains lie within a few yards of Dion Fortune`s in the municipal cemetery at Glastonbury.

Some sixteen years older than Dion Fortune, there is no hint of any romantic attachment between them, but at their first meeting an instinctive rapport was set up as they intuitively realised that their future destinies in this life coincided.

He was a mystic as much as an occultist, and provided the nucleus for the Christian element in the threefold strand of the Mysteries as developed in the Inner Light system. The other two elements were Hermetic philosophy and magic on the one hand, and the Elemental contacts of what was called the Green Ray on the other.

When they met, Dion Fortune had been experimenting with techniques of mediumship for some time. As a result of which she had excited the interest of Frederick Bligh Bond, famous for his clairvoyantly assisted archeological excavations at Glastonbury Abbey. He had been engaged in this work as far back as 1907, long before Dion Fortune came on the scene, although he only revealed the psychic source of his discoveries in a book *The Gate of Remembrance* in 1918. The Church of England had now acquired ownership of the abbey ruins and looking askance at such revelations took steps to bar him from all further connection with the abbey. He soon afterwards emigrated to America but not before meeting and working with Dion Fortune for a time in 1921.

He formed part of a culture at Glastonbury which also included such well known local characters as Alice Buckton, proprietor of Chalice Well, and Kitty Tudor Pole, who had been connected with the strange episode of finding an antique glass vessel at Bride's Well, some twenty years before, that was popularly associated with legends of the Holy Graal. The background story of all these people is admirably told in Patrick Benham's book *The Avalonians*.

Alice and Kitty were both known to Dion Fortune, through

their association with the Letchworth Garden City movement, which was also a consuming interest of her parents, Arthur and Sarah Firth. She and Charles Loveday also stayed at Alice Buckton's residential accommodation at Chalice Well from time to time, which is in fact where they met. Dion Fortune also developed a friendship with Bligh Bond's daughter Mary, who designed the dust jacket for her first novel, *The Demon Lover*, in 1927, and was herself a highly psychic artist and author of a powerful occult novel, *Avernus*, much admired by Dion Fortune.

This group of people were all believers in the existence of an inner plane group known as the Company or the Watchers of Avalon, that was centred upon Glastonbury, and included a former abbot and bishop, Anselm, along with various brothers of the abbey community before its dissolution by Henry VIII. Anselm was martyred at the top of the Tor, but the abbey had until then been an important site of national religious aspirations, for it was here, in 1191, that the monks claimed to have discovered the tombs of King Arthur and Queen Guenevere. This gave considerable prestige to the Plantagenets in their struggle to maintain the Angevin empire, which extended from Normandy down through Anjou and Aquitaine, the inheritance of Eleanor of Aquitaine, Henry II's queen and mother of Richard the Lionheart.

This national element of religious stewardship seemed to be a major concern of the Company of Avalon, a fact which is demonstrated by some of the communication that came through Dion Fortune, when working first with Bligh Bond in 1921 and then with Charles Loveday in 1922. Thus, on Saturday 5th August 1922, a date which Loveday later regarded as the start of all their work together, Dion Fortune received the following:

"We have always told you Glastonbury is important. This matter concerns greatly the Church and the people. I who speak am Arnolfus, priest of the church, and give you the priestly blessing. There be many whom you know who still serve, and we have been called the Company of Avalon."

The gist of the communications in this series was that Glastonbury is a place of great mystical and religious importance because it was here that Joseph of Arimathea arrived to spread the Christian message, and had been welcomed by the native Druids, who had been expecting him. It therefore formed the spot of the first Christian church in England, the root of the Celtic church that antedated the coming of the Roman church, and also formed a natural transition from pagan to Christian belief. It was also claimed that there had never been any break in worship at Glastonbury throughout the whole of the Dark Ages.

Salient parts of the message were:
"When the Church first came here it was a Place of Power, and there was peace in the midst. The worship of the Sun passed over into the worship of the Son. The younger of the druids came into the Christian faith; the older did not oppose, for this was ever a place of peace....The old faith gave the land, and the new faith raised the building, and the young men came in, so that there were men who were priests of both faiths. For at heart both faiths are one, and the druids held a tradition of the coming of the wise men from the East; they were heralded by signs and portents, and when they came they were known and welcomed. Therefore here you get the unbroken tradition of the Sacred Fire; there was no conquering, there was reception, and the old faith carried on. And here you have a line of force that strikes its roots in the earth."

The next day they had a further amplification of this, from one who announced himself as Anselm the bishop.

"This church of which we speak is the church of the Britons and therefore concerns Britain. It is a native church, not a foreign church. The spirit of the people of Britain received a down pouring of the Holy Spirit as typified by the symbol of the Graal. As you were told last night, the priests of the Sun expected the priests of the Son, and they held that tradition, and to the Christian church as founded in this isle of Avalon was handed on the apostolic succession of the great worship, Sun, (the Father); the Earth (mother); the Air (child); and the Water (spirit). Therefore you have here that which is nowhere else in Christendom save at Jerusalem; here you have the unbroken line of a national spirit partaking of the initiations of every age of the world's history, and Avalon has never lacked a seer."

This series culminated on August 17th with a vivid evocation of a figure of the Graal appearing over the Tor at night.

"We are met here together for the down pouring of the Power. The Chalice is above the Tor. This is the hour of the Power of the Chalice. Those who look can see it as a crystal cup through which shows the ruby of the Blood, sailing across the night sky above the tower. Let all look who can see the vision, for now again there is power as of old time, and that power is upon us."

From 1923 onwards however, there came a new dimension in their work together, and the opening up of a more Hermetic line of contacts, which included the reception of an advanced body of metaphysical teaching known as *The Cosmic Doctrine*.

There were just three of them in the earliest days, Dion Fortune, Charles Loveday, and a mutual friend who is known to us only as "Edie". They began to attract a small band of associates but were still virtually only a group of friends with likeminded interests when in 1925 they felt the call to join the Christian Mystic Lodge of the Theosophical Society, and their early work as a group was conducted under this banner.

There was a deeper motive to this move in that they, and their inner plane contacts, felt a certain antipathy to the Star in the East movement which had been gaining great momentum in Theosophical circles over the past fifteen years or so. This claimed the coming of a new World Teacher in the form of a young Hindu, Krishnamurti, and was actively supported by the Liberal Catholic Church which had fallen within the Theosophical orbit. There was some concern, quite widespread in occult circles, that this movement was undermining the true Christian faith by interpolation of oriental conceptions. Dion Fortune and Charles Loveday and their friends therefore saw their role in the Christian Mystic Lodge as a guarding of western traditional values within the Theosophical Society itself. Considerable controversy built up about this and by the end of 1927 they felt they had no option but to leave the Christian Mystic Lodge and the Theosophical Society and to launch themselves as a new independent group, known as the Community, (later Fraternity), of the Inner Light.

This included publishing a magazine, *The Inner Light*, and the continuing Christian commitment of the group was demonstrated within its pages by two long series of articles by Dion Fortune. One a sequence of meditations on extracts from the Anglican liturgy, *Mystical Meditations on the Collects*, and the other a commentary upon their reasons for setting up public Sunday services at their headquarters in what they called The Guild of the Master Jesus.

Although the Fraternity was predominantly an occult one in the old Golden Dawn tradition, incorporating a brand of ritual co-masonry inherited from Dion Fortune's first teacher Theodore Moriarty, there was a strong Christian element within its members. In the early days they were invited to choose a dedicated name for themselves, reflecting their aspirations to be Server of some archetypal figure. About half of the membership had chosen either to be Servers of the Master Jesus or Servers of some particular Christian saint, as opposed to those who chose non-Christian figures such as Thoth or Socrates.

Dion Fortune's opening article in the series on the Guild gave some of their reasons for forming it:

"When we first began our work we urged upon our students the need of devotional and religious practices as well as occult ones, and advised them to continue to worship in the churches in which they had been brought up."

However, in the climate of 1930, when both religious and esoteric attitudes were rather more rigid than they have since become, they found themselves obliged to review this policy, coming to the conclusion that:

"Very few places of worship at the present time are meeting the needs of the type of people who find themselves drawn to the study of esoteric science.

"We therefore decided to organise Divine Worship on our own account, for there was an obvious need for something of the kind. We do not ask people who are content with their churches to abandon them; all we are trying to do is to meet the need of those who have not been able to find what they want in any church. We do not represent a new religion, but a different attitude towards the one and only religion which is to love the Lord our God with all our heart and with all our mind and with all our strength, and our neighbour as ourself."

In the articles that followed it was plain however that their attitude toward divine service in what she called "the Church of the Initiates" was a very "magical" one. That is to say, the same approach to religious ritual pertained as to ritual performed in an occult lodge. Thus:

"The aim of a service is to make an atmosphere in which certain spiritual experiences become more readily accessible. To certain souls, spiritual experiences come in the silence of their own hearts, but others are not so gifted; nevertheless, it is possible for those who themselves have access to these spiritual experiences to make, by means of organised worship, an atmosphere in which many who by themselves could not arrive at these experiences, may have a temporary extension of consciousness which enables them to reach up and receive them. Out of such repeated temporary extensions of consciousness, it soon becomes possible to achieve a permanent enlargement of awareness."

Later in the series she expanded upon the technical or magical side of this:

"We are functioning as adepts in a magical ceremony; we are making a channel of evocation. We are not helplessly leaning upon the Good Shepherd but are as skilled craftsmen preparing the work for the Master. Thus are we able to cause spiritual power to manifest itself upon a level of consciousness normally inaccessible to it, and thus give mystical experiences to those who would be exceedingly unlikely to obtain them unaided. The magical links the spiritual with the material. That is its function and its justification."

In going on to review elements in the liturgy of their service she referred back to the very beginnings of her work, and the contacts with the Watchers of Avalon, from whom had been received the words of the opening prayer of their service:

"Oh Holy Jesus, Master of Love and Compassion, we, Thy little children, dedicated to Thy service, approach Thee in faith in the Living Christ, the Unseen Companion of the Heart. Prepare us, O Lord, to drink of the living waters of Life, soon to be made manifest unto us; open our eyes that we may see, and our hearts that we may understand. Make the way plain, O Lord, that we fail not in Thy service.

"May we be a channel whereby Thy Holy Ones may approach the world. May we be a centre of radiation of Thy power. Teach us to travel light, as do all who travel upon the Path; to give ourselves entirely to Thy service; to attune ourselves to Thy will; to suffer gladly for Thy sake; to lay down the small personal life in the great Cosmic Life, and to love with the Love of God."

She went on to say: "For several years before the Guild was formed, this prayer was used each day in morning meditation in the community house, and it has a very deep significance for our Fraternity. When the command was given to set on foot the work which is now known as the Fraternity of the Inner Light, the group of people who were the pioneers were gathered together by chance at Glastonbury, the Holy Centre of these islands, and this prayer was among the communications and instructions that were then received. It was given by one of those who are known as the Watchers of Avalon. Ever since it has been the especial prayer of those who undertook to carry through this work."

We find, however, in the early 1930's some concern being expressed by C.T.Loveday about the low attendances at Guild meetings. This might not come as too great a surprise in so far that the general public in London has a vast choice of types and places of worship, without recourse to a private house in an inner suburb, whilst much of the actual membership lived outside of the metropolis anyway, and would not have found it easy to travel in for a Sunday morning meeting.

In the Spring of 1936 the Fraternity announced a major reorganisation in what was called a "New Epoch" in their activities. The three-fold approach to the Mystery tradition was more formally organised, with Dion Fortune heading up the Hermetic side as Magus of the Lodge, Dr. Penry Evans as head of the Green Ray activities, and C.T.Loveday invested as head of what they called the Church of the Graal.

This institution of a Church of the Graal was no mere semantic change, but signalled a deeper level to the work of the Guild of the Master Jesus. From now on it was intended that it should have a graded structure in parallel to the Lesser and Greater Mysteries of the Hermetic side of things.

It should not be thought that this resulted in the Fraternity being divided into watertight compartments. All were expected to be capable of working along the lines of any of the three traditions. This is confirmed in the records which show Colonel Seymour, (generally regarded latterly as a died in the wool pagan), as well as Dr. Penry Evans and W.K.Creasy, (a future Deputy Warden), actively engaged in consultations on the desired form of structure and training of the Church of the Graal at this time.

Nor was C.T.Loveday by any means a narrow sighted devotional mystic in his approach to the Mysteries, although he had earlier received a mild rebuff from the inner planes for assuming that they had a missionary task to perform in this respect. Their task, he was told, was not to "convert the world" to their own form of Christian belief, but to perform a specialised act of service within the broad context of the national life. This was later succinctly expressed in terms of the Church of the Graal.

"The Church of the Graal does not touch the nation, it touches the initiates. The Church of the Graal is for the few, it is a living mystical Church."

The general lines for the future work were laid down through Dion Fortune's mediumship and make interesting reading, for they link up with later Arthurian work, undertaken after the outbreak of war, when Fraternity meetings and Guild services had to be abandoned for some time.

"The Guild and the Lesser Mysteries are concerned with the redemption of the personality, but the Greater Mystery aspect of the Christian tradition – the Church of the Graal – is concerned with the descent of the Pentecostal power of the Holy Ghost, and the object of adoration in the Church of the Graal is the Third Person of the Trinity, and its sacred symbol is not the Cross but the Cup...

The real key, then, to the Guild is in the Graal and the object of meditation should be the Graal and not the Cross; the descent of the Holy Spirit and not the historical Jesus; the present, not the past nor the future. The Cross is an important symbol and one cannot experience the higher aspect of the Ascension without it, but ...the focus and nucleus of your work should be the Graal – the adoration of the Third Person, not the Second....Therefore teach in your inner group of the Guild the Graal and not the Cross, for from the Graal comes illumination."

Therefore between 1936 and 1940, when outbreak of war brought a stop to meetings and required a further reorientation of the work, a meditation system was developed for those wishing to work along these lines. In some respects it was a foreshadowing of latter day Pentecostal movements within the orthodox churches, from Catholic to Evangelical, although without the more bizarre manifestations of some of these.

The pattern of the meditation system was to start with the Resurrection and Ascension and the descent of the Holy Spirit, "as a wind that bloweth where it listeth" and source of pentecostal fire, leading on to the bringing of the Graal to the Islands of Britain, from whence could develop understanding of all the Graal Mysteries – the removal of the Cup into the care of the Fisher King, its Quest and Vision and so on.

The Church of the Graal differed from the Hermetic side of the Fraternity's work in so far that the devotional and mystical aspect was regarded as primary, and the occult aspect secondary, even though the sacramental services were performed with the same magical dynamics in terms of ritual technique.

Much of the liturgy of the Guild of the Master Jesus has since been published in *The Story of Dion Fortune* by Charles Fielding and Carr Collins, and in many respects it appears to differ little from general church worship. There is a summons to the congregation to seek spiritual contacts, a general confession and absolution, a reading from the scriptures, adoration and divine praise, prayers for that which is needful, and a blessing of the people. However, much also depended upon visualisations performed by the ministrants. The Lector was no mere reader of lessons but an active officer working in magical polarity with the officiating priest. A major part of their work was building a form of the Holy Graal, as a great chalice filled with the Holy Spirit, above the heads of the congregation and slowly descending.

A graded diaconate was formed, distinguished by ribbons of appropriate colour, black or blue or purple, but more importantly duly instructed in the appropriate forms of mystical meditation.

An attempt was made to revive Guild services towards the end of the war but was abandoned, possibly owing to the increased incapacitation of C.T.Loveday, and in the immediate post war years, after his death and that of Dion Fortune, it was not restored. Rather, with a new generation in command, occult and mystical sides of the work were amalgamated at advanced level, following on from Dion Fortune's Arthurian work with her former Golden Dawn mentor Maiya Tranchell Hayes during the early 1940's. In this the Holy Graal figured as an apotheosis of the Arthurian tradition. Much of this, originally issued to members as *The Arthurian Formula,* has since been publicly disseminated in *The Secret Tradition in Arthurian Legend* and developed in various ways outside the ambit of the Society.

By 1961 however much of this had been worked through, within the Society's doors, and a new phase of the group's work was inaugurated that laid more emphasis upon the

Christian and devotional side, and the whole Fraternity now worked at a single unified level. Although the basic ritual work remained much as it had since 1928 and beyond, it endeavoured to embrace all three strands of Green Ray, Hermetic and Mystical traditions into one.

The Green Ray had gone through a sea change in that it now became very much an ecological and environmental concern for the planet Earth, mystically conceived as an entity known as the Planetary Being. This derived from the original *Cosmic Doctrine* material of 1923/5 where it was originally termed the Planetary Spirit – however as it is more an etheric than a spiritual entity a name change was considered appropriate. This was linked to an increased recognition of the Divine Feminine, not so much in terms of Dion Fortune's Rite of Isis of the 1930`s but as a devotion to the Virgin Mary and the symbolic dynamics of the Holy Family in general.

This radical change did not go down too well with some traditionally minded observers. Indeed Francis King, in *Ritual Magic in England* (1970) concluded that the Inner Light could no longer be considered a magical fraternity but had become a heterodox semi-Christian cult. Arthur Chichester, who was currently its Director, seemed quite happy with that definition, if perhaps not with some of the pejorative remarks that accompanied it. In a letter to an editor who planned a new edition of some of Dion Fortune's fiction he eschewed any connection with the word "occult" and with the Golden Dawn tradition, and said that if any labels were required then the Inner Light could probably best be described as an association of "Christian Qabalists". Whilst in reply to a statement of mine that "the emphasis and direction of the work is radically different from that laid down in the late Dion Fortune's day..." he insisted that "...the Group is now again on the lines Dion

Fortune laid down but considerably further along them."

These differences of perception and of emphasis are only to be expected in the life time of any esoteric group that has an extended life over several generations. In much the same way the Theosophical Society has had its public travails, when the Besant and Leadbeater generation, following upon Madame Blavatsky's founding work, developed a new perspective that in time was rejected by a later wave of Theosophists in what became known as the "back to Blavatsky" movement.

Accordingly we find in the Fraternity of the Inner Light a radical change of emphasis as it moved out of Dion Fortune's generation. Arthur Chichester and Rosina Mann, who inaugurated the 1961 change had joined the Fraternity in 1941 and their perspective ruled the lodge until Chichester's death in 1979 and Rosina Mann's retirement in 1990. Following upon that date, a new generation of senior members began to seek a new reassessment of the work in hand, and with Chichester's broad based reforms as a basis, the work of rebuilding a graded system from Lesser to Greater Mysteries has gradually gone ahead, with less likelihood of the unbalance that occurred to precipitate the radical 1961 changes.

We need to be aware that in any serious occult work that is beyond the levels of a metaphysical discussion group, real and powerful forces are at work. This accounts for the demise of a number of erstwhile groups, and recurrent fitful attempts at regeneration of some others. Back of all attempts at high powered work in the Mysteries of the west there is the need for a sound Christian religious basis – a fact that was well realised by such early pioneers as Eliphas Levi and Anna Kingsford to say nothing of the seventeenth century Rosicrucians and Spiritual Alchemists and eighteenth century Martinists.

Something of the dynamics involved was summed up in an earlier communication from Dion Fortune's inner contacts:

"In times of difficulty and danger go on the Mystical Church contacts. Firstly, because therein is protection, comfort and peace, and secondly, because the essence of the Crucified is to translate these forces into power. Avoid the occult in times of difficulty and danger. Cultivate the Christian in those times. For it is the power of the Christ, as he rides the waters, like the stormy petrel - it is the office of the Christ to still the storm. Your Church, therefore, was inaugurated at the beginning of this terrible period to give you the necessary protection, and it has brought you safely through."

It is a continuation of the spirit of such admonition that the futurework of the Inner Light may proceed in confidence, whether or not the same specific forms are used as in earlier generations of the Society's history.

6
CHANGING LIGHT ON THE MEDIUM AND THE MESSAGE

If the millennial year of 2000 was remarkable for anything, one might well be the publication of four related books that bring to light some of the detail of inner plane communication as experienced in the Fraternity of the Inner Light over the years. These are *Dion Fortune and the Inner Light* and *Spiritualism and Occultism* from Thoth Publications, and *Principles of Esoteric Healing* and *Pythoness, the Life and Work of Margaret Lumley Brown* from Sun Chalice Books.

Dion Fortune and the Inner Light reveals the source of much of Dion Fortune's teaching and how she went about obtaining it. Although hinted at in one or two articles in the pre-war Inner Light Magazine, it was not until 1942 that she openly declared the fact that she had cultivated the technique of trance mediumship for most of her occult career.

Spiritualism and Occultism takes a closer look at this specific technique of communication, as revealed in various articles and transcripts of meetings which could not be quoted in full, for reasons of space, in her biography. Her attitude to Spiritualism changed somewhat during her life and this is revealed in some detail, from the full text of her article *Psychology and Occultism* written in 1922 for the British College of Psychic Science, to her notes on a psychic consultation that she had with a Spiritualist medium, Mrs. Methuen and her contact "White Wing", in 1942.

Principles of Esoteric Healing brings to light a whole range of teaching from an inner source that was never revealed except to close associates during the course of her life. That is to say contacts with "the Master of Medicine", which although having their specialised side nonetheless have aspects with a much broader application. Techniques that are described in the narrower context of clairvoyant diagnosis of medical conditions were later used by Margaret Lumley Brown for the more general purpose of making an esoteric review of the aura of any aspirant to higher initiation. From my own experience this could be quite embarrassingly accurate, as well as giving the pabulum for much fruitful personal research on past incarnations and the like.

Pythoness, as its subtitle describes, gives what is known of the life of Margaret Lumly Brown, who virtually took over Dion Fortune's mediumistic function from the middle of 1946. Starting from the startling revelations of her own natural psychism as a result of dabbling with an ouija board in what turned out to be a dangerously haunted house, she eventually found her way to the Fraternity of the Inner Light where she revealed herself to be, in the opinion of some as "probably the finest medium and psychic of this century, although the public never knew her. She raised the arts of psychism and mediumship to an entirely new level and the high quality of communication that came through her has not been equalled." (Fielding and Collins: *The Story of Dion Fortune.*) With the new book, readers will be able to make up their own minds on this score.

And making up one's own mind on these matters is an important part of the whole process – for no psychic or mediumistic communication should ever be taken as an infallible statement from exalted authority. Automatic genuflection to what might well be someone else's subconscious mind, is not the best way to meaningful spiritual enlightenment. Rather is it an abnegation of will and responsibility that can be an open invitation to the opinionated crank or the confidence trickster, or most dangerous of all, the overbearing cult leader demanding implicit obedience from his or her flock.

There can, however, be a certain glamour that is aroused around the concept of communications received by clairvoyant or mediumistic means. However, one does not have to be the seventh son of a seventh son or be of the umpteenth generation of a long line of psychics to gain access to the inner worlds.

When Margaret Lumley Brown retired from active work in the Fraternity a more conscious mode of working was preferred, under the title of "mediation". In practice there seemed to be no great quantum leap from what had immediately gone before. Over the years, a much lighter form of mediumship began to be practised. The prone position favoured by Dion Fortune gave place to a sitting one, and Margaret Lumley Brown seemed able to snap in and out of the necessary subjective condition with very little trouble.

However, steps were now taken to distance forms of inner awareness from any necessary connection with "psychism". This was an initiative undertaken by Arthur Chichester, the Warden at the time, who had himself suffered somewhat from certain preconceptions about the whole subject. I remember him telling me, somewhat wryly, that not long after Dion Fortune's death he had been recommended to lie in a darkened room "to see what he could get" in terms of psychic vision or communication and getting absolutely nothing.

Yet not for one moment should it be thought that he was as insensitive as the proverbial two short planks when it came to inner awareness. I recall that "Charles Fielding" and I used to be delighted whenever there was an opportunity to sit in on any occasion in which he took a major part. This was because there was a sense of presence about him, a charisma of spiritual weight in prepared conditions, that had made him the natural choice as Warden in 1946 despite the possible rival claims of longer serving members of the Fraternity.

He gave an appropriate talk upon the matter in May 1956 drawing attention to the different ways in which people were likely to function in the context of inner plane contact.

"In that function there are two major divisions which can be seen from experience, the receptive and the active – roughly speaking, the clairvoyant and the adept. Though these two roles are not necessarily sharply separated and can even merge into one another, one or other will be dominant and you will find the individual who should be functioning more actively declaring that he or she does not function well receptively, and also the more passive, who observe things only, often fail to take a more active part in dealing with that which they observe.

"In the language we use we are very seldom able to be completely precise. We have to talk of 'seeing things' or 'perceiving things' and that can give rise to the wrong idea...The actuality is the force and as that comes down the planes it complies with the laws of each plane through which it passes and it has to have a body of that plane. Someone may receive suddenly an idea which is the expression of the same force on the mental plane that later the 'clairvoyant' may see on the astral and that eventually, if all goes well, will percolate through to the physical plane and eventuate in some kind of action or concrete understanding of words or even symbolic and talismanic action...There are a number of possible combinations and it would be very unusual to find two people, at any rate in a small group, functioning each in exactly the same way, and the late Dion Fortune who wrote a great deal, very often put her findings in a form that a clairvoyant would use. She was one who was primarily on the line of the adept, but had also trained herself to be some extent clairvoyant and excellently mediumistic...The intuition has a very large part to play."

He returned to the subject in a talk to neophytes in June 1960:

"It is distressing sometimes to read in reports the remarks of those who have 'been aware of nothing'. Who have 'seen nothing'. I have often touched upon this subject, and I touch upon it again, for it is a perennial one. I understand it only too well, and I sympathise, because I have been through it. I know exactly what it is, and I hold out no hope to you except to persevere. Clairvoyance and psychism are not evidence of spiritual progress. If it is in you to be clairvoyant, you may develop it (and may be led astray by it!). If it is not in you, you will use the subtler senses and be the better for it. But I feel that many of the writers of those reports, set on the idea which they have got from their reading that the effects on the subtler planes are apparent as 'blinding flashes' or 'coloured lights' or 'a touch of the hand in the dark', and looking for these, refuse to accept the real signs that they probably have from a higher level of perception, and block, all unwittingly, development along their true lines."

A major part of this receptiveness of course falls into the province of receiving such forces in terms of words, sometimes lengthy communications, associated with a strongly visualised figure of a particular communicator – whether that figure be fact or fiction or archetype of the unconscious. The practical occultist will take what comes at face value in order to let the force flow, and leave theoretical questions until after – the criterion being whether the message received, by whatever means, and from whatever apparent source, seems worth taking note of.

Psychism has always been recognised as susceptible to various kinds of subconscious distortion, and in the light of experience the more conscious or intuitive ways of working are no guarantee against similar problems. The "piggy in the middle", whether medium or mediator, is susceptible to various subtle pressures that are an unavoidable by-product of natural sensitivity – without which there could of course be no inner communication possible in the first place!

In the record of Dion Fortune's mediumship down the years the expectations, and the type and quality of mind of those who were sitting with her, accounts for much of the quality, type and subject matter of any given communication. This is perhaps no more than a demonstration of the results accruing from the old spiritual adage of "being of one mind in one place..." With some of the verbatim exchanges that are quoted in *Dion Fortune and the Inner Light* we have the opportunity to make our own assessment of their assumed reality and source.

Some of these contacts, moreover, gave some mighty strong hints as to how best to find out these things for ourselves. [The page references are to *Dion Fortune and the Inner Light*.]

"Have you yet become familiar with the inner planes? Use the picture method. Try and see us. It makes us so much more real, and when we are real to you we can talk to you so much more easily. It is by building a form on the astral that we contact you. That form has hitherto been built by the consciousness of the transmitter, but if you could build composite forms with the group consciousness you would obtain more definite results, and when each one of you has become accustomed to building a picture in consciousness in group meditation, and of hearing the sound of the voice, you would soon find that you are able to build that form in solitary meditation and hear the voice in your inner consciousness; and the more to whom we can speak, the stronger will the group be.

You will have many problems to solve in the course of your work, but one thing you must always guard, and that is your belief in the Masters, for without that you can do nothing. It is your contacts with them that are the source of your powers as a group, but it is highly desirable that each one of you shall learn to hear for yourselves the voices within, and for that purpose we shall work upon you and visit you individually, and you must try and hear us. You must listen for us and reach out towards us. Visualise us one by one, and call upon us and try to hear the answer. Thus you shall make the contacts for yourselves. For we are real. We are what we claim to be, and the proof lies in the power. If you doubt the power, invoke it and watch it work. When you come to these meetings come in faith, for it is your faith that makes the communication possible, and without it we cannot come through." [p.89]

"The Masters as you know them, and the Hall of Initiation, are all imagination. I did not say the Masters were imagination. I said the Masters, as you know them; and I imagine myself, and you imagine me, and between us we make a simulacrum on the astral which enables us to get in touch with each other. What I am you cannot realise, and it is a waste of time to try to do so, but you can imagine me on the astral, and I can contact you through your imagination, and although your mental picture is not real or actual, the results of it are real and actual.

"The Masters, as they are supposed to be in popular would-be esoteric thought, are pure fiction. Learn to write novels on the astral because it is by creating a true-to-type thought form that you get in touch with that which transcends thought; and as long as you are a concrete consciousness you will have to use the astral to touch the abstract, and it is the laws of the astral thought form that are taught in esoteric science." [pp. 90-91]

"When you come to meet your pupils, visualise myself. Thereby I shall be enabled to pick up contact with you. Then, putting aside all voluntary endeavour, allow the teaching to flow through you.

"Let come what will come. You will find it a mistake to over prepare your lessons; and I will give this advice – do not refer to it on the day on which you give it. Then, when you come to meet your class, learn to listen mentally to the atmosphere of that class. You will soon learn to sense it and, like the conductor of an orchestra, you will soon be able to pick out the sounds of the individual instruments of the orchestra...

"Always remember this, that when you stand up to speak on esoteric matters, you are standing up in the name of the Masters, and if you allow it, the Masters will come and speak through you, and you will find yourself giving utterance to things you have never known. Learn to trust to the impulse, and do not be afraid to give utterance spontaneously to things that are coming through you." [p.174]

This last advice, given to a student supervisor in 1929, may seem to call for a lot of faith - in oneself as well as the master. It does, of course, take two to tango. And this is the difference between ordinary extempory creative expression off one's own subconscious resources, and making a genuine link with an objective inner plane communicator. However, it is likely that you need to practice on your own before your efforts possibly attract an inner contact to the dance. This is the basic reason for the meditation discipline in any esoteric school.

From my own ounce of experience, if contact is really wanted from the inner side then contact will inevitably be made, although it can come in unexpected ways.

I was well into my fifties before any regular and systematic communication as a means for teaching others came from an identifiable inner plane source. Even then it was not of my own seeking. It began with a recurring imaginative picture, allied to an impulse that I did not welcome very much, which was to write a novel starting from that scene. As a professional publisher of some experience I saw no commercial or cultural value in attempting such a Herculean and unrewarding task. But eventually with somewhat bad grace I sat down to write up the pictures that came into my head along this theme, if only to prove once and for all that the whole thing was really pointless.

The initial subjective picture was of myself sitting in the bar of a seaside hotel in the midst of some revellers who were about to depart for a fancy dress party of "vicars and tarts". (I make no admission to any unconscious symbolism here!). When they left I was left alone in the bar with a figure in somewhat old fashioned army uniform who was vainly trying to feed coins into a slot machine. He asked me to come to his aid, and upon examination it appeared that his difficulty was caused because in his hands he had only pre-decimal coinage – big old pennies bearing the heads of George V, Edward VII or Queen Victoria.

Striking up a conversation he said that some gentlemen wished to see me in an upstairs room. To my surprise and no little annoyance the room number he gave was the one that I knew I was staying in – Number 7 (again no symbolism intended). Assuming it to be some kind of high pressure salesmanship scam I rushed upstairs to have it out with them. On throwing open the door I found myself face to face with a couple of senior Masters of the Wisdom, patiently waiting to see me. With no further ado they simply started to talk, and after some little difficulty I began to write down what they said. Thence came about a considerable body of teaching that formed a core of instruction for groups I was later working with.

Once I had been conned into realising I could do it, it was relatively easy to continue. The only difference from ordinary writing being that it came through at twice, sometimes nearly three times, the speed at which I can normally write - about 1200 as opposed to 500 words an hour.

The point I wish to make, however, is that I do not consider the ability to be particularly rare. It is no more difficult than telling a story nor is it necessarily connected with long esoteric training. My article, *The Wells of Vision,* (published in the *Inner Light Journal,* (Vol 17 No 4 AE 1997) and the book of the same name gave an example of two handed working along these lines where the most relevant experience of the person who was working with me and taking the lead was probably as a teacher telling extemporary stories to children. The difference between the normal use of the imaginative faculty and its esoteric use lies principally in the spiritual intention or motivation, and the use of esoteric associations and symbols.

The imagination of the Qabalistic student is considerably helped by the traditional attributions that are applied to the Spheres and Paths of the Tree of Life, where it is simply a question of making up a story using the relevant building blocks that are laid to hand. Here however one should not be overawed by an authoritative attitude that tends to be enshrined in older books, or proclaimed by armchair pundits whose grasp of speculative theory considerably outweighs their practical experience. Traditional attributions may be useful as guides but should not be inhibitors of free association.

Laying out Tarot cards and making a story from them is no bad method for freeing up the imagination and developing an esoteric sense. They do not always have to be applied to the comparative trivia of telling fortunes, and some hints along these lines may be obtained from my own *The Magical World of the Tarot* and *Tarot and Magic (a.k.a. The Treasure House of Images.)* From thence one can open the gates of vision into a whole range of spiritually authentic fantasy and eventually instruction.

Whether the latter comes from your own subconscious, super-conscious, an Angel of the Tarot, or one of the Ascended Masters is a comparatively minor point – if you invest time in the practice then you should be rewarded by increasing quantity and quality of spiritual insight, which after all is the aim and even definition of Initiation.

7
THE LADY OF THE LAKE

One of the key points of Dion Fortune's work on the Arthurian legend was that the Lake was an astral region and the domain of faery women, and so it may be useful to examine the role of that very important person, the Lady of the Lake.

At the beginning of his reign, it is from a Lady of the Lake that the young King Arthur receives his empowerment, in the form of the magic sword Excalibur. At the end of his reign it is to a Lady of the Lake that the sword is returned.

Thus the powers reserved within the Lake are those that grant sovereignty to the king in his appointed mission, as ruler of Logres and the Company of the Table Round. It is therefore worth considering just what and where this Lake might be, and who its denizens are.

Local traditions give various locations for specific lakes, from Dozmary Pool in the southwest peninsula of England to Bala Lake in Wales, but whilst local traditions of sacred sites may be helpful in giving anchoring points to the mind, all such locations are but representations of a reality that encompasses them all. This reality we might call the Other World, an inner Earth behind the physical world we know. Some occultists have called it the "astral plane" (a comparatively modern expression) but in more traditional terms and in this context it perhaps best known as the World of Faery or Elfland.

Let us turn to the young Arthur who has been taken into the tutelage of Merlin shortly after the beginning of his reign. Arthur has successfully proved his rightful kingship by pulling a sword from a stone and then defeating in battle the concourse of old kings, all reluctant to accept the credentials of this unknown upstart.

There remained a particularly redoubtable character by the name of King Pellinore whom Merlin advised was best left alone. However, Arthur, with the impetuosity and vainglory of youth, insisted in engaging him in personal combat. As a result the sword he had drawn from the stone to prove his kingship was broken and he found himself in mortal danger. As he lay disarmed and pinned under the giant-like ancient king, Pellinore was about to cut off his head when Merlin intervened and cast the old warrior into a deep sleep.

After spending three days in a hermitage having his wounds dressed and reflecting upon his folly Arthur rode off with Merlin, a sadder and wiser youth, and now without a sword. Let Sir Thomas Malory take up the tale in the 1st Book of his *Le Morte d'Arthur.*

"And as they rode, Arthur said, I have no sword.

No force, said Merlin, hereby is a sword that shall be yours, an I may.

So they rode till they came to a lake, the which was a fair water and broad, and in the midst of the lake Arthur was ware of an arm clothed in white samite, that held a fair sword in that hand.

Lo! said Merlin, yonder is that sword that I spoke of.

With that they saw a damosel going upon the lake.

What damosel is that? said Arthur.

That is the Lady of the Lake, said Merlin; and within the lake is a rock, and therein is as fair a place as any on earth, and richly beseen; and this damosel will come to you anon, and then speak ye fair to her that she will give you that sword.

Anon withal came the damosel unto Arthur, and saluted him, and he her again. Damosel, said Arthur, what sword is that, that yonder the arm holdeth above the water? I would it were mine, for I have no sword.

Sir Arthur, king, said the damosel, that sword is mine, and if ye will give me a gift when I ask it you, ye shall have it.

By my faith, said Arthur, I will give you what gift ye will ask.

Well! said the damosel, go ye into yonder barge, and row yourself to the sword, and take it and the scabbard with you, and I will ask my gift when I see my time."

This sword plainly belongs to the Lady of the Lake. *"That sword is mine!"* From all that follows we may regard it as the gift of sovereignty, which has to be returned in the end. Not only that, it is subject to certain conditions, that apply to many transactions between this and the Other world. In this instance the young Arthur has virtually presented her with a blank cheque.

Much has been made of the "divine right of kings", and whether or not Arthur's sovereignty was ultimately divine command, it is plainly shown to be here as a right that is mediated and bestowed from the inner Earth.

At the conclusion of his reign Arthur knows very well that he has to return the sword to its rightful Other world owners, from whom he holds it only upon licence. His companion Sir Bedevere does not have such an appreciation of the values at stake – his views are moulded by common sense expediency. Who could possibly benefit by his throwing away such a precious and historical artefact, he asks himself, with all too human duplicity. Three times the grievously wounded Arthur tells him to throw the sword back into the lake before he finally does so. Then the reasons for this seemingly irrational order become apparent:

"...and then he threw the sword as far into the water as he might; and there came an arm and an hand above the water and met it, and caught it, and so shook it thrice and brandished, and then vanished away the hand with the sword in the water."

The return of the sword was also a sign to the Lady of the Lake to come to fetch him and bear him away to Avalon, rather than to mortal death. It is thus no wonder that Arthur cavilled so grievously at Bedivere's prevarication:

"And when they were at the water side, even fast by the bank hoved a little barge with many fair ladies in it, and among them all was a queen, and all they had black hoods, and all they wept and shrieked when they saw King Arthur. Now put me into the barge, said the king. And so he did softly; and there received him three queens with great mourning; and so they set them down, and in one of their laps King Arthur laid his head. And then that queen said: Ah dear brother, why have ye tarried so long from me? Alas, this wound on your head hath caught over-much cold. And so then they rowed from the land, and Sir Bedivere beheld all those ladies go from him."

From the fact that one of the mourning queens greeted the king as her brother we may assume that it was his half sister Morgan le Fay, whose name suggests that she was herself of faery blood, or at any rate familiar with the ways of faery. Malory also gives a short list of ladies within the ship in Chapter Six of Book 21.

"...but thus was he led away in a ship wherein were three queens; that one was King Arthur's sister, Queen Morgan le Fay; the other was the Queen of Northgalis; the third was the Queen of the Waste Lands. Also there was Nimué, the chief lady of the lake, that had wedded Pelleas the good knight; and this lady had done much for King Arthur, for she would never suffer Sir Pelleas to be in no place where he should be in danger of his life; and so he lived to the uttermost of his days with her in great rest. More of the death of King Arthur I could never find..."

Although much of Arthurian legend comes from Celtic sources it is the Anglo-Saxon Layamon, writing *Brut* (his version of Geoffrey of Monmouth's *History of the Kings of England*), in Middle English alliterative verse, who is the first to specifically mention elves:

"Arthur was wounded wondrously much. There came to him a lad, who was of his kindred; he was Cador's son, the Earl of Cornwall; Constantine the lad hight, he was dear to the king.

Arthur looked on him, where he lay on the ground, and said these words, with sorrowful heart: 'Constantine, thou art welcome; thou wert Cador's son. I give thee here my kingdom, and defend thou my Britons ever in thy life, and maintain them all the laws that have stood in my days, and all the good laws that in Uther's days stood. And I will fare to Avalun, to the fairest of all maidens, to Argante the queen, an elf most fair, and she shall make my wounds all sound; make me all whole with healing draughts. And afterwards I will come again to my kingdom, and dwell with the Britons with mickle joy.'

Even with the words there approached from the sea that was a short boat, floating with the waves; and two women therein, wondrously formed; and they took Arthur anon, and bare him quickly, and laid him softly down, and forth they gan depart.

Then was it accomplished that Merlin whilom said, that mickle care should be of Arthur's departure. The Britons believe yet that he is alive, and dwelleth in Avalun with the fairest of all elves; and the Britons ever yet expect when Arthur shall return. Was never the man born, of ever any lady chosen, that knoweth of the sooth, to say more of Arthur. But whilom was a sage hight Merlin; he said with words – his sayings were sooth – that an Arthur should yet come to help the English."

Layamon also mentions elves being involved in the circumstances of Arthur's birth.

"...Ygaerne was with child by Uther the king, all through Merlin's craft, before she was wedded. The time that was chosen, then was Arthur born. So soon as he came on earth, elves took him; they enchanted the child with magic most strong, they gave him might to be the best of all knights; they gave him another thing, that he should be a rich king; they gave him the third, that he should live long; they gave to him the prince virtues most good, so that he was most generous of all men alive. This the elves gave him, and thus the child thrived."

In this respect they were acting in the time honoured tradition of "fairy godmothers" who bring gifts at the birth of a particular human being. Although in some stories this can also be curses, if they have not been invited or have suffered some slight from the human family.

However, in Arthur's case, they seem to have been somewhat more than this, for in Layamon's version, they took the child away, just as in other branches of the story Merlin was said to have taken him.

This accords with a tradition, not just of faery "changelings", babies swapped in cradles according to later medieval folk belief, but of human children of a particularly high destiny being taken to be educated in faery realms before returning to the world to take up their mission in the human kingdom. In the Arthurian legends this type of child is signified by a name that refers to the Other world Lake – thus Lancelot du Lac, or of the Lake.

For details of this we need to turn to the "enfances" of Sir Lancelot, and also his cousins Lionel and Bors, who shared this experience. The last named was eventually one of the Grail winners. These stories are contained in the old French prose romances known collectively as the Vulgate cycle (c.1215-30) or "the prose Lancelot", from which most later versions, including Malory, depend. It is, however, a vast compilation, almost a medieval soap opera. Thus Malory felt obliged to leave out many long passages, including the details of the faery childhood or Lancelot and his cousins.

They are available to us, however, in a modern English translation, under the title of *Lancelot of the Lake* although here again, some sections, including the faery childhood have been summarised rather than translated in full. A more detailed version of this period in Lancelot's life is also to be found in the German version of a lost French romance, *Lanzelet* (c. 1194-1203) by Ulrich von Zatzikhoven, although here the good Swiss confuses the Lady of the Lake with a mermaid! She rules however over a thousand ladies dressed in silk and brocade in a land where the climate is always like the month of May, within a castle upon a spherical crystal mountain. The castle was of gold and had a diamond gate and nothing within it ever aged, nor was it ever disgraced by anger or envy. There the young Lanzelet was taught to sing and to play all sorts of stringed instruments and by the "mermen" to use sword and buckler, to jump and wrestle, to throw stones, spears and darts with accuracy and to shoot with bow and arrow.

In the Vulgate *Lancelot,* the lake into which Lancelot disappears is known, at least by implication, as the lake of Diana, the pagan goddess of the woods. Lancelot is the son of King Ban of Benwick and his wife Helen, who suffer grievously when their kingdom is lost to their rival, King Claudas of the Waste Land. As if these tribulations were not enough King Ban is thrown from his horse, and in the resultant confusion the baby Lancelot is put down on the ground close by the lake, and in danger of being trampled by loose horses as the queen and her companions rush to the stricken king's side. The queen falls into a swoon at the sight of her husband's death, but as soon as she recovers her first thoughts go to her child.

"Then she leapt up again and went running down the hill, her hair dishevelled and her clothes torn. When she approached the horses, beside the lake, she saw her son, unswaddled and out of the cot, and saw a damsel holding him stark naked in her lap, clasping and pressing him very gently to her bosom, and kissing his eyes and mouth repeatedly."

The morning was cold and the queen begged the damsel to put the child back to his crib for he had hardship enough to face, having just been orphaned of his father. The damsel however, made no reply, but as the queen approached, stood up and holding the child in her arms went straight to the lake and jumped in. They were not seen again, and the despairing queen entered a nunnery.

The damsel who took the child is named as Niniane, and described as a faery, and an associate of Merlin, who lives in the lake with other faery knights and damsels – although the location is described as being not really a lake but a magical illusion.

Only Niniane knows Lancelot's name, the others referring to him as the Handsome Foundling, or the King's Son or the Rich Orphan. As befits a child who will one day become "the best knight in the world" he is of extreme beauty and skill in all the knightly virtues. Eventually the time comes when he proves too much of a handful for his tutor to handle, who begins to suspect his mortal and kingly origins.

His two cousins Lionel and Bors are brought to join him, they being sons of his uncle King Bors of Gannes, who died shortly after hearing of the death of his brother Ban, Lancelot's father. Their childhood has been spent in the somewhat ambivalent wardship of King Claudas of the Waste Land and now in their early adolescence they are imprisoned in a tower. The Lady of the Lake commands one of her damsels, named Saraide, to rescue them.

Saraide arrives at Claudas' court at the feast of Mary Magdalene accompanied by two squires, each of whom is leading a greyhound. The two boys have been allowed to be present at the feast, although Lionel, the older and more headstrong of the two, secretly carries a knife with which he plans to stab King Claudas.

Saraide puts a gold clasp around the neck of each of the boys, which renders them immune to wounds from weapons. She also places a chaplet of herbs upon their heads which has the effect of exciting the boys to vigorous action. So when Claudas proffers Lionel a cup, instead of drinking from it, the boy strikes the king with it, laying him out cold. The two boys seize the royal regalia on display, Lionel taking the sword and Bors the sceptre. In the ensuing confusion Saraide leads them toward the door. Dorin, King Claudas's son, tries to stop them, but with blows from sword and sceptre they strike him down and kill him.

Claudas, having come to himself, rushes after them but by her magic Saraide turns the boys into the semblance of greyhounds and the two greyhounds into the appearance of the boys. She throws herself before Claudas and the hilt of his sword splits her face open, permanently scarring her. While she remonstrates with him he is astonished to find that he was apparently only trying to attack two dogs. He has the real dogs led away and locked up, to be dealt with later, thinking them to be the boys.

Saraide now leads the real boys, in the form of greyhounds, back to the lake where they are restored to their true appearance and made welcome by Lancelot and the Lady of the Lake, where they are later joined by their human tutors.

At the age of eighteen Lancelot receives from the Lady of the Lake detailed instruction in the rights and obligations of knighthood. She also provides him with the necessary arms and equipment. It is notable that all are in the traditional faery colour of white. Besides his sword, she gives him a white hauberk, a silvered helm, a snow-white shield with a silver boss, a lance with white shaft and head, and a big strong swift horse as white as the driven snow. For the celebration of his knighting she gives him a robe of white samite, a cloak lined with ermine, and a tunic lined with white sendal.

Thus they set off a week before Midsummer's Day, or the Feast of St. John, with forty white horses ridden by servitors all dressed in white, accompanying Lancelot and his cousins. The Lady of the Lake herself is also dressed in tunic and cloak of white samite, trimmed with ermine, and riding a little white palfrey, with its saddle housing of the same white samite as the her clothes and reaching to the ground, its bridle, breast strap and stirrups of silver white, with a saddle of ivory carved with tiny figures of knights and ladies.

Crossing the English channel, they land in worldly terms at what appears to have been Weymouth, and arrive eventually at Camelot. There, meeting King Arthur and his entourage as if by chance in open countryside, it is arranged that the king will make Lancelot knight.

Here a certain matter of earthly and faery protocol has to be negotiated. It was the custom for the one who conferred knighthood to provide the new knight with all his apparel and accoutrements, but the Lady of the Lake insists that upon this occasion, they should be the ones in the faery colour of white that have been provided by her. The King agrees, and Lancelot then bids farewell to the Lady of the Lake, who is much moved by their parting.

"There is much I would say to you, but I cannot, for my heart is wrung, and I cannot speak. Go now, good and fair, gracious and sought-after by all, loved by all women more than any other knight – I know you will be all these things."

With that she kissed him warmly on the mouth, the cheeks, and the eyes, and rode off, so grief-stricken that no one could make her speak.

Lancelot also took his leave of his cousins Lionel and Bors for the time being until such time as they would be knighted. He himself was taken into the care of Arthur's court, where he soon met the Queen herself, where obviously each was much taken by the other at first sight,

"The queen looked at the youth a great deal, and he at her, whenever he was able to do so discreetly. He wondered where such great beauty as that which he saw in her could come from. The beauty of the Lady of the Lake, he thought, or of any other woman he had ever seen, could not compare with this. He was certainly not wrong to esteem the queen above all other women, for she was the lady of ladies and the fount of beauty; yet if he had known her merits, he would have been even more eager to look at her, for no woman, rich or poor, could match her worth."

Of the subsequent relationship between Lancelot and Queen Guinevere much has been written, and much is of moment to the development of the Arthurian story, but does not immediately concern us. This version is of course a variant upon the tradition wherein Lancelot, already a knight of

Arthur's court, is sent to collect Guenevere from her father prior to her marriage to Arthur. Whatever the circumstances, there is evidently a great rapport instantly set up between them.

Part of this may be because the stories seem to be dealing with paragons - paradigms of grace and beauty that seem almost superhuman and to verge upon the ideal standards of the world of faery. Elsewhere in the Vulgate cycle Guinevere is cited as one of the three most beautiful women in the world, the other two being Helen of Troy, and Heliabel, the sister of the Grail knight Percivale.

There is a separate tradition, indeed, that suggests that Guinevere herself was of the faery rather than the human kind, her name deriving from the words "woman in white".

Another tradition included in Malory is of the Lady of the Lake being married to one of the Round Table knights, Sir Pelleas. This would seem to be part of a tradition of faery ladies taking mortal lovers. Malory cites Pelleas as one of only six knights who ever got the better of Gawain in combat.

It is a strange story that has parallels in the Tristan and Iseult cycle and also with the troubadour traditions of courtly love. Sir Pelleas is completely besotted with a lady, the fair Ettard, who spurns his love, despite his having won a tournament in which five hundred knights contested for her hand. So smitten is he with her beauty that he allows her knights to capture and ill use him time and time again simply so that he may be taken to her castle and accorded a sight of her. None of this softens her heart and she seems to hate him all the more for it.

Eventually Gawain comes across the situation and volunteers to help Pelleas by interceding for him with the lady. However, when he meets the fair Ettard he too is smitten by her beauty, and she with him. They are found sleeping together by Pelleas, who refrains from violence, but leaves his sword athwart their throats in token that he has discovered their treachery. In his desolation at this double betrayal he goes grieving through the woods where he is met by the Lady of the Lake. Learning of his story, she takes pity on him and throws an enchantment upon both Pelleas and Ettard.

As a result of this enchantment, Ettard at last falls passionately in love with Pelleas, but Pelleas is now caused to hate Ettard as much as she formerly hated him. This ends in Ettard dying of unrequited love whilst Pelleas himself is taken in marriage by the Lady of the Lake. The marriage of a knight to a faery lady is found in certain Breton lais and also as a legend in certain medieval families, of which one of the most celebrated is of the faery Melusine to the founder of the Lusignan dynasty who later provided two kings of Jerusalem and founded and ruled over the kingdom of Cyprus for some three hundred years. An interesting preamble to these faery marriages, which occur with the Lady of the Lake and Pelleas, with Melusine and Raymondin of Lusignan, and with her mother Pressine and King Elinas of Albany, is that the first contact is always made when the hero is suffering great grief.

Under the tutelage of the Lady of the Lake, Pelleas becomes a knight of King Arthur's Round Table, although understandably his relations with Gawain were always somewhat strained. The Lady of the Lake also took care to ensure that Pelleas never found himself on the opposite side to Sir Lancelot in any joust or tournament. This may have been because Lancelot, being the best knight in the world, was certain to win, but also possibly because both Lancelot and Pelleas were so close to her heart, the one as her former ward and surrogate son, and the other as her human lover.

The Lady of the Lake appears at certain other times in the life of King Arthur besides the beginning and the ending of his reign. She arrives just in time to save him when his sister Morgan le Fay attempts to kill him by exchanging Excalibur and its scabbard for a false one, giving the true one to her favoured knight of the time, Accalon of Gaul. When the two fight, Arthur begins to get the worst of it but fortunately the Lady of the Lake, aware of what is going on, arrives and restores the true Excalibur to Arthur who promptly vanquishes his half-sister's knight.

One of the strangest episodes concerning the Lady of the Lake is when she returns to demand the granting of the wish that Arthur promised her upon receiving Excalibur.

It follows hard upon another sword test when a lady comes to Arthur's court saying that she is an emissary from the Lady Lile of Avelion, which some might have presumed to be the Lady of the Lake (of the Isle of Avalon). She seeks assistance from a knight of the court, but the only knight who can be acceptable will be one who can draw the sword from the great scabbard that she bears concealed beneath her cloak. All the knights of the court attempt this feat, including Arthur himself, but all of them fail. In the end a poor knight steps forward who has been kept a prisoner for more than a year awaiting trial for alleged murder of another knight. This poor knight, whose name is Balin, succeeds in drawing the sword.

He declines to return the sword to the maiden however, who then warns him that he will live to regret possessing it, for with it he will kill the best friend he has in the world and the sword will also cause his own destruction. Thereupon she departs.

However, before Balin can leave on his quest the Lady of the Lake arrives to demand the gift that is owed her by Arthur's promise. This turns out to be Balin's head or else that of the maiden who brought the sword to him.

Arthur is thrown into a considerable quandary. On the one hand to renege on his Otherworld promise. On the other to foreswear the human duty of hospitality and protection that he owes to guests at his court.

A web of accusations and counter-accusations do little to help him in this matter, which might be regarded as a test of judgement and rulership. The Lady of the Lake says that the knight unlawfully killed by Balin was her brother, and furthermore that her father had been slain by the maiden. Balian, for his part, accuses the Lady of the Lake of being a duplicitous enchantress, responsible for the death of many good knights, and who has caused his mother to be burnt at the stake.

While Arthur stands bemused Balin takes the law into his own hands and strikes off the head of the Lady of the Lake. This immediately places him beyond the pale and he is banished forthwith by Arthur. Indeed a knight of the Round Table, Sir Lanceor of Ireland, with Arthur's permission, pursues him to exact vengeance but is slain himself.

Merlin arrives to try to throw some light upon this complicated scene. He confirms that the maiden who brought the sword is a false enchantress, but that Balin will suffer the doom that is placed upon the magic sword. This turns out to be the case for eventually he meets with his own brother, Balan, and as anonymous champions of rival claimants, after a protracted battle they kill each other in combat. This however is not before Balin has delivered the Dolorous Stroke – using one of the Grail Hallows, the Lance, to wound the Grail King in the thigh. This is the commencement of the Grail cycle which eventually causes the dispersal of the Round Table fellowship before the last days.

Much of high portent hangs around this series of incidents, which appear in Book 2 of Malory, for along with the alleged interment of the Lady of the Lake, (a counterpart to Merlin's later interment by a damsel of the Lake), there are references to damsels being bled for the custom of a castle, (a theme which appears later in the Grail Quest), and also the strange interment and the fashioning of images of twelve ancient kings by Merlin each illuminated with a perpetual light.

However, whatever the truth of this tangled skein of high and low enchantment, the Lady of the Lake has not been slain by being beheaded, for she reappears again in later stories. Notably in an incident in Book 9 where King Arthur almost loses his life in the Forest Perilous but for the intervention of Sir Tristram, who is brought to the scene by the Lady of the Lake. Once again a treacherous woman, the Lady Annowre, had got hold of Excalibur and was about to cut off Arthur's head with it. Tristram kills the two knights who were attacking Arthur and the Lady of the Lake cries to Arthur not to let the lady escape. He pursues her and cuts off her head, which the Lady of the Lake claims, tying it by the hair to her saddle bow. To what purpose is left to our imagination.

The Lady of the Lake's last appearance at Arthur's court is in the somewhat flaking latter days when Guenevere is accused of attempting to kill a knight with a poisoned apple. The Lady of the Lake arrives to announce the queen's innocence and to reveal the real guilty party.

Thus the Lady of the Lake and her companions represent a beneficent faery world behind the Arthurian court. They may also appear in other guises, not specifically as faeries, but as initiators as for example in the story of Gareth of Orkney, in Malory's 7th book where the Lady Linet spurs on the young knight with carping criticism while he undergoes the various tests with the different adversaries, from thieves in the forest and defenders of a ford through to the blue, green and red knights. The knight Breunor le Noire has a similar lady appropriately called Maledisant who in the end becomes his wife with transformed name and function as the Lady Beauvivante!

In coded form, many of these adventures are instructional manuals for the processes of higher initiation.

8
DION FORTUNE AND THE BRITISH MYSTERIES

Dion Fortune, besides being one of the most prominent occultists of her generation, an active leader of groups from 1922 through to 1946, was also one of the most versatile. She described her work to be like a rope of three strands.

One was the magical tradition of Hermetic philosophy. This was expressed in her association with a branch of Co-Masonry, founded by her first teacher, Dr Theodore Moriarty, and then successively with the Alpha et Omega and Stella Matutina Temples of the Golden Dawn tradition as well as founding her own ritual group, the Fraternity of the Inner Light.

The second was Christian mysticism. This was expressed through her early association with Frederick Bligh Bond and contact with the Watchers of Avalon at Glastonbury, then through becoming President of the Christian Mystic Lodge of the Theosophical Society. From this the Guild of the Master Jesus came to birth which later developed a more esoteric graded structure as the Church of the Graal.

Then there was what she liked to call her Green Ray work. This included a broad sweep of traditions ranging from Elemental and Nature contacts, through Power Centres, Sacred Sites and Ley Lines, to various forms of the Arthurian Tradition.

Actually, there was also a fourth line of work, that saw little publicity in her life time. This was Esoteric Medicine which she developed in conjunction with her husband Dr Thomas Penry Evans and later with other sympathetic members of the medical profession. The full extent of this has only recently come to light through the discovery of files in the archives of the Society of the Inner Light. However, most is now available in the public domain under the title of *Principles of Esoteric Healing*.

With an occultist who has as wide a spectrum of activity as this it is understandable if many people prefer to approach her from one angle only, the one that accords with their own views. It is partly for this reason that she is nowadays considered something of an icon in the neo-pagan movement. I cite as my authority for this Professor Ronald Hutton in his monumental book *The Triumph of the Moon*. I have no quarrel with this assessment of her role, as long as it is realised to be only a part of the whole woman, and her contribution to the occult movement of the 20th century. For the moment, however, let us concentrate upon just this one side of her various activities.

Let us go back then to her involvement with Frederick Bligh Bond at Glastonbury. I should say that she was not directly concerned with Bligh Bond's famous archeological work on Glastonbury Abbey that had been assisted by psychic means, rather to the horror of the church authorities. Bond had commenced this in 1907, when Dion Fortune was hardly out of school. She came along very much towards the end of Bligh Bond's association with Glastonbury, in 1923, just a couple of years before he decided to up stakes and leave for America.

During the previous two or three years she had been trying to develop powers of mediumship and had become proficient enough at this to do some work with Bligh Bond. The immediate consequence of which was contact with an inner group calling itself the Company of Avalon. This resulted in a script that emphasised the importance of Glastonbury as being a site for the old Druidic religion. According to this, the Druids had been expecting a mission from the East announcing the coming of a new religion. This eventually came to pass and the two sets of disciples, the pagan and the Christian, met and co-operated with each other. This of course is the gist of the Joseph of Arimathea legend from which branched various elements eventually connected with the Grail tradition.

This combined Christian and pagan element was an important feature of Dion Fortune's early work at Glastonbury. We might perhaps quote from salient parts of it to illustrate its depth and commitment.

"When the Church first came here it was a place of power, and there was peace in the midst... The younger of the Druids came into the Christian faith; the older did not oppose, for this was ever a place of peace. For, think ye, it was a stronghold of the old faith. How could a small band of pilgrims, men of peace, not of war, have landed and built and dwelt, if those who held the island had not permitted, and welcomed, and given as a gift the land on which the church stood? The old faith gave the land, and the new faith raised the building, and the young men came in, so that there were men who were priests of both faiths. For at heart both faiths are one, and the Druids held a tradition of the coming of the wise men from the East; they were heralded by signs and portents, and when they came were known and welcomed. Therefore here you get the unbroken tradition of the Sacred Fire; there was not conquering, there was reception, and the old faith carried on. And here you have a line of force that strikes its roots in the earth."

This historical legend was accompanied by certain topical prophecies. Remember that the horrendous experience of the First World War had been over but five years previously. With the ending of this war it was felt that another age would come, bringing in powers of the spirit so that the old centres would awaken, re-open and revivify.

Where the passing age had seen the building of the abbey in bricks and mortar, and its eventual destruction, now an unseen edifice was being built on the same site, with invisible walls. Strong in spirit, raised by a great company of just men made perfect, who loved and served the spirit and faith of England. These inner guides sought to meet those in the flesh who still served and remembered the ancient glory that was Glastonbury.

As far as they were concerned, Glastonbury was unique, for there had never been a break in the tradition of worship from one epoch to another. From the Elemental powers of the Worship of the Sun to the Spiritual powers of the Quest of the Grail there was a complete run through of power. It was, in short, a place of spiritual regeneration — as befits its ancient description as "the holyest erthe in England". There was here, something which could be found nowhere else in Christendom save at Jerusalem, the unbroken line of a national spirit partaking of the initiations of every age of the world's history. Avalon had never lacked a seer.

Within three years of making this contact, Bligh Bond had gone his way, Dion Fortune had established herself at Glastonbury, having bought a plot of land at the foot of the Tor and constructed a chalet upon it, known as Chalice

Orchard. It was actually up on the Tor itself that she and her groups experienced a powerful elemental contact at Pentecost of 1926.

They had, apparently, a little while before been conducting some meditation or little ritual invoking the Element of Air when, walking upon the Tor, they were suddenly taken up with a feeling of ecstasy which set them whirling spontaneously in an impromptu dance. Then they saw a friend rushing across the fields below, who raced up the hill to join in their revel. In the whirling dance a repetitive chant seemed to beat through into consciousness, which they rendered into words, a kind of affirmative mantram:

"The wind and the fire work on the hill –
The wind and the fire work on the hill –
    The wind and the fire work on the hill –
Evoke ye the wind and the fire.
And then:
Earth and water are friendly and kind –
    Earth and water are friendly and kind –
        Earth and water are friendly and kind –
The sun and the fire work on the hill –
Hail to the sun and the fire."

All this became interspersed with various injunctions about the power and people of the Elemental Kingdoms. Fire and Air were associated with the Tor. Water with Chalice Hill at its foot. And Earth with Wearyall Hill across the other side of the town where Joseph of Arimathea had first planted his thorn staff that took root as a tree.

"The place is guarded,
    A ring of fire is about you,

    And the freedom of the hill is yours.
For this is a hill of Fire
    And the forces of Fire are about you
      And the protection of Fire is upon you.
Do not think about the Nature forces,
    Feel with them —
      Move with them —
        Sing with them —
    Do not be afraid of them. You need them,
      For they are on the Power side of things,
  And without the Elemental Forces, you have no Power.

You have no Power to give expression to your desires unless it be the will of the Lords of the Elements, for they hold the Gates, and the Gates open to admit to the Inner World, and you can go in by the grace of the Lords of the Elements.

They are your friends if you can rule your own Elemental nature.
    They share with you the holiness of Elemental nature.
You must make them respect you, and you must respect them.
    You must love them, and they will love you.

Those who love the Elements, and those whom the Lords of the Elements respect and trust, shall be entrusted with the Force of the Elements. And the Power of the Elements shall be as a flame among men.

    As a rushing tide —
      As a mighty wind —
        And still as the rocks.

You shall sweep things aside as a Fire if the Lords of the Elements ride with you.

The Kings of the Powers of the Air shall ride with you.
> And the stability of the depths of the Earth shall guard you.

Where our friends are there is purity and power.
> Where the waters sweep out to the endless horizon, spaceless and timeless for ever, there shall be strength.
> Where our people are,

there is strength and wealth and wisdom.
> As the rocks are rich, as the rocks are strong, so the deep things are wise."

It was upon this tide of Elemental power that she founded what was to become her Fraternity, with a headquarters in London as well as the Glastonbury site. And characteristically with the many sided ambience of her destiny, this Elemental contact ended with a Christian evocation, a somewhat unexpected and somewhat unorthodox one – so it may prove something of a stumbling block to the more conventional type of Christian or the more narrow type of pagan alike.

"Come from the depths of your Elemental Being and lighten our darkness.

Come in the name of the White Christ and the Hosts of the Elements. Come at our bidding and serve with us the One Name above all Names –

> The Lover of men and of the Elemental Peoples –
> > The Great Name – of JEHOSHUA – JESUS.

He who said as he descended into the Underworld:
> There shall be no night where my people are –
> And the night shall be as day in the light of the eternal fire
> And there shall be peace where my people are –

>The peace of the heights above the winds.
>And there shall be purity.
>Fire and Air –
>Fire and Air –
>For Power to serve the Master."

As was explained to them a little later by one of their inner contacts, in the three days between the Crucifixion and the Resurrection, the Christ descended to the Underworld to preach to the spirits in prison. Amongst these were spirits of the Elemental kingdoms who had not been touched by the higher spiritual contacts. To them also, as with man, he gave the power to become the sons and daughters of God.

In this, I suggest, is the heart of the tradition of the Adept being an initiator of the Elemental Kingdom. Man being possessed of an immortal spark of divinity that can confer immortality upon Elemental beings, creations of the created, who might otherwise be destined only to have individual existence for the space of an evolution.

There are of course many types and grades of Elemental Being as there are types and grades of men. As was also further explained to Dion Fortune and her group of friends:

"Learn to be on terms of friendship with the Lords of the Elements. Always conduct your dealings with Elementals through the Lords of the Elements. The Lords of the Elements are beings of lofty intelligence – mighty Intelligences. They, like you, are dedicated to the Masters. They will not serve you. Never make the mistake of commanding their obedience, but rather, as brethren, praying their assistance as servants of the One Master."

By 1927 Dion Fortune had founded a school, the Fraternity of the Inner Light, and the importance of Glastonbury was reflected in a number of essays she wrote for the newly founded *Inner Light Magazine.* These were eventually published in book form as *Avalon of the Heart.*

Here she evokes the various aspects of Glastonbury, commencing with the road to Avalon from London, the Great West Road, along which she must have travelled a number of times in the 1920's in the side car of a Harley-Davidson motorcycle driven by her colleague and general factotum, Thomas Loveday.

"The road winds, for it is an ancient way, worn by wandering feet that sought firm ground and good wine rather than a direct route. Above, on the hill-tops, lie the fortresses of primitive man; the earthworks that guarded his wonderful towns, and the terraces called shepherds' steps from which he fought the wolves. The setting sun shines low among the apple orchards. The smoke of the peat that comes from the Bridgewater marshes smells sweet in the damp of the evening. The houses are all of grey stone, for we are within hauling distance of the Mendips. Great three-horse teams, harnessed in single file, block the way as the timber wagons go home. Low platforms at the roadside await the clanging milk lorries that charge down the narrowest lanes of the dairying country."

This Somerset countryside is perhaps largely lost in our own days, some eighty years later, but there remains beneath it the deeper Avalon she evoked. The Avalon of Merlin, Avalon of the Graal, Avalon of the Keltic Saints, even Avalon and the traditions of the sunken land of Atlantis.

She also records one of her earliest reminiscences of Glastonbury, where, in 1920, she was present at the first performance of Rutland Boughton's *The Immortal Hour.* This musical play, based upon a libretto by Fiona McLeod, I am pleased to say has been recorded on Compact Disc. If anyone wants to feel the hair stand on the back of their neck through the power of the ancient Faery contacts I can recommend purchasing and playing it at an appropriate time in a secluded place. (It is produced by Hyperion, catalogue number CDD22040.)

It obviously had a great effect upon Dion Fortune, for she records that the performance: "timed to fit in with the exigencies of the local buses and trains, began at sunset. The first scene started with broad daylight shining in through the uncurtained windows of the Assembly Rooms. But as it progressed the dusk drew on, till only phantom figures could be seen moving on the stage and the hooting laughter of the shadowy horrors in the magic wood rang out in complete darkness, lit only by the stars that shone strangely brilliant through the skylights of the hall. It was a thing never to be forgotten."

It was in Glastonbury also that she set to work to write her main book of occult philosophy *The Mystical Qabalah* upon which two generations of students of her school have since been trained. Having completed this theoretical work, she turned her mind to trying to exemplify some of its principles by practical example. But occult secrecy was taken very seriously in those days, - so seriously that it all but strangulated many otherwise burgeoning groups in the Golden Dawn tradition. She therefore turned her thoughts to fiction.

She had already written a number of short stories and a somewhat blood and thunder novel on general occult lines,

The Secrets of Dr. Taverner and *The Demon Lover* in the 1920's. But her sequence of novels published soon after *The Mystical Qabalah* in 1935 are in a very different league. They comprise *The Winged Bull, The Goat-foot God,* and *The Sea Priestess,* with its sequel, published post-humously, Moon Magic. It is the content of these novels that I think enthuses most of her pagan admirers, however, as she later revealed, they were each based upon Qabalistic principles.

In a series of articles in the *Inner Light Magazine* she explained some of the thinking and motivation behind her occult fiction. She said she wrote by the same method that she used in writing an occult ritual. Here she reveals an important element of occult teaching and practice in the Western Esoteric Tradition.

It remains the assumption of many outsiders or elementary students of the tradition that the Hermetic Tradition, rather like Freemasonry, is composed of a few set rituals, of which one may not change one jot or one tittle lest one impair their efficacy.

However, as Dion Fortune says: "A practising occultist is constantly making his own rituals for whatever purpose he may have in hand; in fact it is one of the tests of a properly trained initiated that he can make a ritual for a given purpose, and that it will produce results."

Of the principles of ritual making, she says, that: "although a great deal of secrecy has been observed with regard to them, they are scattered through innumerable published works and unpublished papers. Finally, I gathered them all together and published the essence of them in my *Mystical Qabalah*. Those who know that book will see that my novels are Qabalistic works."

I think this point worth emphasising, as I have seen it assumed that the novels are a great paon of paganism, unrelated to anything that went before or afterward in her life. However, such narrowness of vision is in the eye of the beholder rather than the wand of the practitioner.

However, there is much of pagan interest within her fictional work. Much indeed has become commonplace now, but was somewhat novel in her day. For instance when her Celtic heroine Ursula Brangwyn sets up a retreat for herself it is in the mountain fastnesses of Snowdonia.

On the other hand, the hero of the book, Ted Murchison, of Viking extraction, works best at a retreat on the North Sea coast of Yorkshire. This is all in accord with a theory, according to Dion Fortune, that:

"If a line is drawn from St. Aldhelm's Head in Dorset, to Lindisfarne off the coast of Northumberland, all the Keltic contacts are found on one side of it, and all the Norse contacts on the other. The Keltic Ursula is contrasted with the Norse Murchison, and on this turns much of the inner magic of the book...Up on the flanks of Snowden Murchison is at a disadvantage; he is not contacted with the native magnetism of the place...[but] as soon as Murchison crossed the Humber when bringing the car from Wales, he felt as if he had 'come into his own'. The whole book...is full of such touches as this, not put in deliberately, but coming out unconsciously. ."

It may be of interest to note that Dion Fortune had similar views about various districts of London. With reference to the villain of the piece, Hugo Astley, she writes: "The scene of Astley's noisome abode is laid in north-east London because there are some very sinister spots round that district; others may be found in Pimlico, and if I had known as much about occultism as I do now, Bayswater would not have been my first choice as a centre."

For those contemplating acquiring real estate with a view to constructing a magical temple some other hints may be worth recording: "Bloomsbury is a district in which it is easy to do magic, and so is Chelsea; whereas in neighbouring Fulham, it is very up-hill work."

This conjures very evocative images of the young Dion Fortune's early experiments in practical occultism. However, there is a great deal in what she says that has since been evocatively expressed in, for example, the novels of Peter Ackroyd or the works of Ian Sinclair, to say nothing of less publicised researches of Chesca Potter around King's Cross, or of others about Greenwich. There is indeed as much occult power available in a city as in any remote sacred site, if of another type and mixed with a variety of impurities and even degradations.

Dion Fortune certainly had a soft spot for the area around the British Museum, perhaps, as she says, because of the multiplicity of old gods housed there. And also for the south bank of the Thames, which served as a location for Lilith Le Fay Morgan, her heroine in *Moon Magic* (even if the building was based upon "The Belfry", now a restaurant I believe) north of the river, in Belgravia. A converted warehouse on the south bank was also the evocatively described location of the hero of one of her romantic crime novels, *The Scarred Wrists,* written under her pseudonym of V.M.Steele.

It was at the Belfry that she instituted semi-public performances of her Rite of Isis. This, however was less directly related to the Mysteries of Britain than to a mixture of Greek and Egyptian sources.

Her novel, *The Goat-foot God* celebrates the Rites of Pan, and although Pan is of course a Greek god, he is nonetheless a universal one who rules over certain aspects of nature everywhere, not least in the British Isles.

Aspects of place are important in all her novels — not least in *The Sea Priestess,* where the sea priestess's temple was inspired by the ruins of an old fort and gun emplacement, on that rocky headland just south of Weston-super-Mare called Brean Down. I have always found the ruin and the rocks beyond it quite evocative, although it may have been converted to a cafeteria by this time. The Sea Priestess might have been a match for all kinds of problems of wind and weather but it is doubtful if she would have been able to stand her ground against the caravan parks and holiday camps that now stretch along the coastal road from Burnham on Sea.

It is for this reason that I prefer to leave sites such as Stonehenge to the coach parties bussed in to the barbed wire ramparts of National Heritage, and seek my native contacts in places the Tourist Board has never heard of. Gone are the days, when in my youth, it was possible to wander the stone circles alone.

However, popularity has its place, and from its small beginnings in 1927 Dion Fortune's organisation grew from strength to strength until within ten years it had become a fashionable esoteric centre.

In 1938, for example, her headquarters had played host to a series of debates upon the esoteric tradition graced by London literati. These included Christina Foyle, of the famous bookshop, and occult writers and novelists such as Elliott O'Donnell, Claude Houghton, Berta Ruck and Marjorie Bowen. These were jointly chaired by Dion Fortune and the academic Bernard Bromage.

The lecture programme for Spring 1938 gives some indication of the breadth and depth of the work in progress. Four talks by Dion Fortune on "The Esoteric Tradition", "Ceremonial Magic", "The Esoteric Doctrine of Sex and Polarity", and "The Doctrine of Magical Images". A joint lecture by Dion Fortune and Colonel Seymour, on "Methods of Occult Training", (including a practical demonstration), and three lectures by Seymour illustrated with magic lantern slides on "A Reconstruction of Isis Worship" and "A Reconstruction of the Worship of Pan", including chanting by Dion Fortune.

The series was commenced and concluded by her husband, Dr Tom Penry Evans, on "Spiritual Healing" and "The Mental Factor in Health". The Fraternity's activities excited interest in the whole London esoteric world at this time. Even Aleister Crowley and a couple of his acolytes turned up on one occasion.

All this was brought to an end by the outbreak of war, when travelling and public meetings became difficult if not impossible.

From September 1939 until midway through 1942 Dion Fortune ran things mostly by correspondence. By a series of weekly letters she kept in touch with scattered members and sympathisers, organising concerted meditation sessions at a distance.

I have seen her criticised for being too nationalistic in this phase of her work. It seems to be forgotten by anyone who thinks this way, or who feels uncomfortable with the concept of patriotism, that the country was at war and fighting for its life at this time. London was under constant aerial bombardment, and there can be few teachers in the annals of occultism who have found it necessary to give instruction on how best to meditate when being subjected to the threat of high explosive and incendiary bombs.

Her letters during this period, extracts from which have since been published as Dion Fortune's *Magical Battle of Britain,* display a courageous and humorous woman making the best of very difficult circumstances, at a time when in one month alone 6350 civilians were killed and 8700 injured as a result of the bombing.

They had begun by visualising angelic forces patrolling the coasts of the British Isles but then certain images began to formulate to her meditation group at this time, constellating about certain key Arthurian figures, in the form of a triangle that linked three coloured spheres, of red, blue and purple.

In the red sphere a mailed rider began to formulate, grasping a sword, and was identified with King Arthur. In the blue sphere a seated figure appeared, holding a diamond sceptre or rod of power, who was identified as Merlin. And in the purple sphere was seen a figure of the Christ holding the cup of the Holy Grail. By the end of April 1940 this triangle had transformed into a three dimensional pyramid with a figure of the Virgin holding the cup in the purple sphere, whilst the Christ rose to the golden apex of the pyramid. If any of you prefer to see these latter figures as forms of the Goddess and the Son of Light, then you are very welcome to do so.

By June of 1940 this whole complex had transformed into a cavern beneath Glastonbury Tor, illuminated by a golden equal-armed cross, a mystic rose, and the rainbow colours of Lords of the Rays, from whence a passage led up inside the sacred hill to a tower housing a library, a chapel and a watch-tower. In a sense this was an internal affirmation of what had been experienced externally in the visions of 1926.

None of this, I have to say, stopped the roof being blown from their headquarters in September. However, they drew consolation from the fact that no severe structural damage had been done to the walls and that a statue of the Risen Christ had not been dislodged from the altar. With such small mercies, people used to console themselves in those days.

In a few weeks they were able to move back in, after the roof had been rendered waterproof.

There was also a deeper side to her Arthurian work. This came about through joining forces again, after a period of twenty years, with her erstwhile Golden Dawn teacher, Maiya Tranchell-Hayes. They undertook an intensive series of workings between April 1941 and February 1942 and a long series of trance communications resulted in a document known as the *Arthurian Formula* which formed the staple of the Fraternity's work for some years to come, indeed up until almost 1960.

It was based upon the somewhat startling premise that the Arthurian tradition, predated not only medieval romance writers but also the Keltic traditions. That it was a folk memory of certain dynamics that pertained to a civilisation that colonised the western seaboards of Europe, in Ireland,

Cornwall, Britanny even before the erection of the stone circles. Whether or not one calls this Atlantis is a matter of convenience and convention. To do so is liable to render one being accused of lacking in education if not intelligence. However, it remains an enduring tradition in esoteric circles, from Madame Blavatsky to Rudolf Steiner, so perhaps we do best to regard it as a myth. A myth that should be taken seriously, and not according to the short sighted dictionary definition of being an invented falsehood. Let us call it an enlightening fiction, if we will.

In practical occult work, as in experimental work of any investigative discipline, it is results that count. If they go counter to established theoretical principles, then that is too bad for established theoretical principles.

Let me say simply that I undertook a weekend workshop based upon the Arthurian Formula, at Hawkwood College back in 1981, and the results of it reverberate to this day. I had little idea that I was setting off an esoteric time bomb that had been primed by Dion Fortune and Maiya Tranchell-Hayes forty years before.

I need hardly add that the gist of the work is still capable of considerable development, but that may be for a future generation, not my own. At least however I have managed to put much of the material into the public domain, under the title of *The Secret Tradition in Arthurian Legend.*

And so it is, that the torch gets handed on from generation to generation. And it is the same flame, the same light, that is passed on by each of us.

We none of us can claim any credit save for how we preserve and pass on that which we have received, hopefully making the flame a little brighter as we do so.

Dion Fortune stands however, in my opinion, as the greatest of all fire raisers. Greater than the rest of us, by virtue of the breadth of her vision and abilities during her relatively short active life as a teacher. She is one, who to my mind, is in the line of the great company of the Vestal Virgins of the ancient world, who kept the Sacred Fires of the Mysteries, and of the Hearthfire of the State, burning through their selfless dedication. We who follow, can only aspire to raise our penny candles to her star.

THE ESOTERIC STUDIES OF
THE SOCIETY OF THE INNERLIGHT

DION FORTUNE, founder of The Society of the Inner Light, is recognised as one of the most luminous and significant figures of 20th Century esoteric thought. A brilliant writer, pioneer psychologist and powerful psychic, she dedicated her life to the revival of the Mystery Tradition of the West and she left behind her a solidly established knowledge of many systems, ancient and modern.

This special edition brings together two immensely valuable classic books which make the complex foundations of psychic development accessible to all readers.

ESOTERIC ORDERS AND THEIR WORK examines how occultists have jealously restricted admission to their secret societies and schools and shrouded their practices in mystery. Dion Fortune here uncovers the workings of these secret organisations and describes their operations in detail.

THE TRAINING AND WORK OF AN INITIATE shows how, from their ancient roots, the Western Esoteric Systems have an unbroken tradition of European initiation that has been handed down from adept to neophyte. This book indicates the broad outlines and underlying principles of these systems in order to illuminate an obscure and greatly misunderstood aspect of the Path.

ISBN 0 - 85030 - 664 - 7

APPLIED MAGIC is a selection of Dion Fortune's writings on the practical applications of magical and occult techniques. Written from the point of view of a gifted psychic, they provide invaluable and suggestive pointers to anyone intent on increasing their inner awareness.

ASPECTS OF OCCULTISM looks at nine specific aspects of the Western Mystery Tradition, including God and the Gods, Sacred Centres, The Astral Plane, The Worship of Isis, Teachings Concerning the Aura, and the Pitfalls of Spiritual Healing

ISBN 0 - 85030 - 665 - 5

THE ABBEY PAPERS

The Abbey Papers, which comprise this book, came to Gareth Knight over a period of ninety days, apparently stimulated by some editorial work he had been doing upon the War Letters of Dion Fortune, subsequently published as Dion Fortune's Magical Battle of Britain.

He had not particularly sought to set up as a channel of communication in this way but the initiative seemed to come from within, nagging away at him compulsively, much as some poets are pressured by their muse, until he sat down and did something about it – if only to prove that all was nonsense or of no great consequence. To his surprise it all started to flow quite readily and the fact that it now appears in print means that at least he and the publishers feel that there is something within it all that is worth sharing.

ISBN 1 899585 80 X

THE WELLS OF VISION

The chapters in this book consist of articles that appeared in the Inner Light Journal, house journal of the Society of the Inner Light, between Spring 1997 and December 2001. They have as a common theme, aspects of Gareth Knight's own magical work and experience.

Awen, the Power in the Magical Cauldron first appeared as a Foreword to the book Awen, the Quest of the Celtic Mysteries by Mike Harris [Sun Chalice, Oceanside, Cal. 1999]

Qabalah and the Occult Tradition was first given as a talk on 30th May 1999 to a conference on Kabbalah and the English Esoteric Tradition, at the Ashmolean Museum, Oxford, organised by the Kabbalah Society.

ISBN 1 899585 65 6

THE MAGIC RAILWAY

Fairy story or esoteric pathworking - following a long tradition!

The lives of the Selby children are threatened with disruption as their Media World parents part. They are consigned to the care of the fearsome Gerda in Notting Hill. The previous owner has mysteriously vanished. Mr Pretorius it seems was a great traveller on an extra dimensional magical railway from Nothing Hill Gate. Together they follow in his tracks and the youngest, Rosy, finds herself the centre focus for a life and death struggle involving the Grail and the restoration of order and balance to the world.

ISBN 1 899585 61 3

GRANNY'S PACK OF CARDS

There is much more to the Tarot than a curious game as Rebecca and Richard discover. Illustrated. Publication 2003

A children's fantasy story by Gareth Knight. Richard and Rebecca meet the Joker of their granny's magic pack of cards and, assisted by his dog, meet many of his friends on a hair raising cycle of adventures that takes them to many strange worlds such as the Mountains of the Stars beyond the Gates of Time and thence to the Wondrous Island at the Heart of the Rainbow.

Any correspondence with the figures they meet and the pictures in the Tarot pack are entirely coincidental – but we all know
what coincidences are – and they receive much fascinating instruction on this and that by characters as diverse as the Star Maiden and the Great Emperor, having evaded such dangers as the DarkTower and the Desert Reapers. All ends happily with their triumphant return to Myrtle Cottage having made some
acquaintance with their True Names and Essential Goodnesses.

ISBN 1 899585 85 0

DION FORTUNE TAROT CARDS

Strangely the Society of the Inner Light did not produce a Tarot pack although its symbolism is a feature of her classic MYSTICAL QABBALAH.

Now at last is a version of the Tarot in line with Dion Fortune's understanding and that of the Order of the Golden Dawn. All the suits of the Lesser Arcana have been illustrated with images reflecting their symbolism from classical times to the present day. The explanatory booklet also gives guidance on Tarot pathworkings, which are valuable psycho/spiritual exercises and a very positive use of the Kabbalistic Tree of Life.

ISBN 1 899585 73 3

THE DEMON LOVER

Young and innocent Veronica is taken on as Mr. Lucas' secretary though he has other plans for her... Without fully realising just what is going on Veronica finds herself involved in the work of a mysterious sinister male-only magical Lodge. In spite of Lucas' ruthless exploitation she falls in love with him and becomes an accessory in his occult workings.

To try to protect her from the wrath of the Lodge because of her unlooked for and unwanted attraction, Alec Lucas is immersed deeper and deeper into the darkness of the Underworld, ever struggling to free himself from many hells.

This was Dion Fortune's first novel, based on real characters and experiences. It offers many insights not only into the inner nature of the Mysteries and the dangers of Black Magic but also defines aspects of the sacred nature of love.

When it was published the Times Literary Supplement considered it to be 'exceedingly well-written', and it has stood the test of time.

ISBN 1 899585 30 3

THE ESOTERIC PHILOSOPHY OF LOVE AND MARRIAGE

Dion Fortune's basic esoteric textbook on the psychology of love and relationships give a simple explanation of the universal factors governing interaction between masculine and feminine from the 'lowest' to the 'highest' level of the Seven Planes.

This sensitive and authoritative account, written by a distinguished woman who combined uncanny intuition with "hands on" psychological experience clearly states the principles of polarity underlying all relationships between men and women with insight and sensitivity.

These principles remain as true today as when this classic guide was first published, at the time it was fully realised that a formal marriage contract or ceremony would in no way neutralise or diminish the tensions of sexual incompatibility caused by temperamental differences, conflicting goals or destinies.

Sex is a function, not an ideal and there are other factors producing harmony or otherwise. The feminine is 'positive' on the Spiritual Plane and that of the Emotions. While the masculine tends to be more 'positive' on the Mental and Physical planes. In a proper union, these aspects are harmoniously complementary so the relationship remains in balance. Where these aspects are unrecognised and are denied free expression, disharmony can often result. Needless to say the physical expression through sex will also suffer, since attitudes derived from the 'higher' levels control or inhibit the 'lower' physical aspect.

THE ESOTERIC PHILOSOPHY OF LOVE AND MARRIAGE also includes Dion Fortune's teaching on some of the esoteric principles behind abstinence and asceticism, contraception and abortion.

ISBN 1 899585 25 7

THE COSMIC DOCTRINE

Seventy two years ago a remarkable event took place beginning at the Vernal Equinox in Glastonbury. For very nearly a year Dion Fortune received communications from the Inner Planes concerning the Creation of the Universe, which later became a classic.

THE COSMIC DOCTRINE remained a closely guarded secret until 1949 when a closely edited version was privately printed since Dion Fortune's successor considered the original "a most dangerous book".

It is now available for the first time in its entirety in the original text in this definitive edition.

This full text examines the no man's land where Science and Magic interact. The Cosmology of the "Big Bang" and Chaos Theory running parallel to the evolutionary process. Each Human Spirit volunteering to learn the lessons and acquire the experience going hand in hand with the physical Universe.

But a cryptic warning accompanies these clearly outlined concepts; this book is designed to train the mind rather than inform it. In other words it is intended to induce a particular attitude both to the inner and outer world. Most must realise, words can hardly describe the immensity of the Cosmic creative process and the manifold complexity of our planetary and atomic systems under the jurisdiction of the Solar Logos.

THE COSMIC DOCTRINE further illustrates the true nature of Good and Evil which man generally views from his own highly subjective and very personal perspective. There are further insights into the interaction of positive and negative polarity within the universal scheme of things.

Besides the Creation of the Universe and the evolution of Mankind the COSMIC DOCTRINE has much to teach about Natural Law, the evolution of Consciousness and the Nature of Mind.

Illustrated with diagrams by one of Dion Fortune's closest collaborators.

ISBN 1 899585 0 52

GLASTONBURY, AVALON OF THE HEART

Dion Fortune first visited Glastonbury while Bligh Bond was still uncovering its past with his amazing psychic investigations into the Abbey ruins. It was at Glastonbury also that she received her first major and dramatic Inner Plane contact in Chalice Orchard close to Chalice Well.

Later she acquired the plot of the land and established a retreat, where it had all happened, under the shadow of the Tor.

AVALON OF THE HEART is her personal account of the love affair with Glastonbury that drew her back repeatedly across the years.

Her description remains one of the most evocative and poignant accounts of this wild yet holy place; a power centre polarising with distant Jerusalem and linking and harmonising the Christian way with the primaeval and pagan past.

She includes as a background time honoured legends of Joseph of Arimathea, the Grail and Arthur the King with special insights since she, more than any other, re-established these long overlooked historic matters of the Isles of Britain with special authority.

AVALON OF THE HEART is besides, both lyrical and poetic, recapturing the timelessly inspiring mood of Glastonbury, as she knew and loved it.

To pilgrims of the Aquarian Age her account is a precious reminder of Britain's heritage and its deep roots in the past. Not only that, but a gateway to the future.

With black and white illustrations by Peter Arthy.

ISBN 1 899585 20 6

MACHINERY OF THE MIND

"One of the shortest and clearest of the many popular books on modern psychology which have been published."

When she was barely twenty Dion Fortune was working in London just before the 1914-18 War as a lay analyst and so obtained first hand practical insights into that aspects of the human condition. Her subsequent esoteric work placed a heavy emphasis on the unwisdom of embarking on the Mysteries without thorough inner preparation. In a perfect world this would mean that candidates for initiation would present themselves with a clean bill of psychological health.

machinery of the mind was considered sufficiently important to form part of the standard background reading for the Study Course offered by the Society of the Inner Light that Dion Fortune founded.

ISBN 1 899585 00 1

THE MYSTICAL QABALAH

Dion Fortune's THE MYSTICAL QABALAH remains a classic in its clarity, linking the broad elements of Jewish traditional thought - probably going back to the Babylonian Captivity and beyond - with both eastern and western philosophy and later Christian insights.

Dion Fortune was one of the first Adepts to bring this 'secret tradition' to a wider audience. Some before her often only added to the overall mystery by elaborating on obscurity, but her account is simple, clear and comprehensive.

The Qabalah could be described as a confidential Judaic explanation of the paradox of 'the Many and the One' - the complexity and diversity within a monotheistic unity. Whereas the Old Testament outlines the social and psychological development of a tightly knit 'chosen group' culture, the supplementary Qabalah provides a detailed plan of the infrastructure behind the creative evolutionary process.

A major limitation of the Authorised English Version of the bible is the translation of the many Hebrew God-names by the single name "God". THE MYSTICAL QABALAH devotes a chapter to each of the ten schematic 'God-names', the qualities or 'Sephiroth', which focus the principle archetypes behind evolving human activity: the Spiritual Source; the principles of Force and Form; Love and Justice; the Integrative principle or the Christ Force; Aesthetics and Logic; the dynamics of the Psyche and finally, the Manifestation of life in earth in a physical body.

THE MYSTICAL QABALAH works in a profoundly psychological way. Its lessons for the individual are invaluable and this book is a must for all who feel drawn to getting to know themselves better so that their inner world and their outer world may be at one.

ISBN 1 899585 35 4

PSYCHIC SELF-DEFENCE

When she was twenty, Dion Fortune found herself the subject of a particularly powerful form of psychic attack, which ultimately led to a nervous breakdown. With the benefit of hindsight, and her experience as a practising occultist and natural psychic, she wrote Psychic Self Defence, a detailed instruction manual for protection against paranormal malevolence.

Within these pages are amazing revelations concerning the practices of Black Lodges, the risks involved in ceremonial magic, the pathology of non-human contacts, the nature of hauntings and the reality behind the ancient legends of the vampire. In addition, the book explores the elusive psychic elements in mental illness and, more importantly, details the methods, the motives, and the physical aspects of psychic attack - and how to overcome them.

Dion Fortune was born Violet Mary Frith in LLandudno, 1880. A brilliant writer and pioneer psychologist, she became increasingly interested in her own psychism and the study of magic. She went on to become a powerful medium, mystic and magician and devoted her life to her role as priestess of Isis and founder of the Society of the Inner Light, until her death from leukaemia in 1946.

ISBN 1 899585 40 0

MOON MAGIC

BEING THE MEMOIRS OF A MISTRESS OF THAT ART

The Sequel to The Sea Priestess

The manuscript of this novel was found among the author's papers and tells the return of Morgan Le Fay, the bewitching, ageless heroine first met with in The Sea Priestess. This fiction classic is last in the series planned by Dion Fortune and which was designed to impart much of the teaching of the Western Esoteric Tradition.

The story centres round an enchanting love affair that will appeal both to those searching below the surface for the principles and tenets behind the Western Esoteric Tradition as well as to the connoisseur of good fiction. Both will be fascinated by this modern tale of Magic and Mystery, with the Old Gods as Archetypes and demonstrating their power to affect us in the world today.

For a mysterious cloaked figure continually haunts the dreams of Dr.Robert Malcolm, a caring, successful yet unfulfilled medical practitioner: The image grips his imagination until it becomes close to a reality, ever moving softly ahead of him at dusk through the damp London streets, and mirroring the reflection of his nightly dreamscape.

...Until late one fateful evening, the substance of his dreams enters his surgery, unheralded yet in person... the unforgettable and eternally attractive Morgan Le Fay.

Then as Priestess of Isis she gradually returns him to the Natural World he has for so long abandoned. Taking on the painstaking task of renewing his soul and masculine power within the confines of her secret magical temple.

As time goes on, the chemistry between them stabilises into a clearly defined polarity and Dr. Malcolm is transformed in the process.

MOON MAGIC is a classic account and exploration of the interplay between masculine and feminine, anima and animus and a searching study of human and superhuman relationship.

ISBN 1 899585 15 X

THROUGH THE GATES OF DEATH

The text explains the stages in the natural process of dying that every departing soul passes though from this world to the next. The correct attitude being that death is simply birth into a new form of life and therefore to be regarded as a joyful and positive event.

Dion Fortune further sets out the requisite states of mind as well as the necessary actions by which those closest to the deceased can speed and smooth their passing and which should accompany the natural progression of death, laying out, burial and mourning.

This handbook has proved to be an invaluable aid and comfort to all confronted with bereavement, whatever their situation; whether seeking to do what is best for a departed loved one or to widen their own perception to bridge the mysteries between Life and Death.

ISBN 1 899585 10 9

THE GOAT FOOT GOD

Desperate and wretched after his wife's death at the hands of her lover, Hugh Paston turns to the Ancient Mysteries in search of Pan to re-establish and confirm his own manhood. With another seeker, Paston acquires an old monastery intending to convert it to a temple of Pan. The building is troubled by the spirit of a fifteenth century prior, walled up for his heretically pagan beliefs, who also searched for the goat-foot God. This entity plans to take over Paston's body to pursue his unremitting quest and it is left to Mona, Paston's partner's niece to help solve the problem of human love in this case, when in reality man and woman become representatives of the God and the Goddess.

'Shoots with remarkable success at a most ambitious target.' – The Guardian.

ISBN 1 899585 06 0

THE MAGICAL BATTLE OF BRITAIN

Immediately following Germany's invasion of Poland, which resulted in Britain's declaration of war, Dion Fortune, the founder of Britain's foremost magical order - The Society of The Inner Light - initiated a magical programme designed to thwart the expansionsist intentions of the Third Reich, and thus the invasion of Britain.

Now, fifty years on, those instruction papers have been released from the archives of her school. Accompanied by a commentary from Gareth Knight, himself a student of Dion Fortune's fraternity, these teachings offer the reader an astonishing insight into the workings of a genuine esoteric school and their - until now - hidden yet significant contribution to the Nation's war effort.

ISBN 1 - 899585 - 00 - 1

THE SECRETS OF DR TAVERNER

Based on real people, this collection of short stories, presents Dion Fortune's teacher (said to be Dr Moriarty) with herself cast in the role of his assistant, Rhodes. Taverner uses his abilities to cure the severely mentally disturbed by esoteric techniques. By technical work on the inner planes he frees his patients from frustration, misery and worse. Rhodes, though just a learner, becomes more and more engrossed in the work until the day she overreaches herself, just like the Sorcerer's Apprentice; only just escaping terror-drenched disaster.

Each story highlights a psycho-esoteric aspect; vampirism, astral journeying, karmic repercussions, demonic interference; and this edition includes a previously unpublished story.

ISBN 1 899585 02 8

THE SEA PRIESTESS

In Dion Fortune's own words; "This book stands on its own feet as a literary Melchizedek."

It is a book with an undercurrent; upon the surface a romance; underneath a thesis upon a theme; "All women are Isis and Isis is all women."

Further, it is an experiment in prose rhythms which beat upon the subconscious mind in the same way as the Eastern Mantra, which, because they are archaic, speak to the archaic level of the mind whence dreams arise.

Dion Fortune considered with some reason, that the psychological state of modern civilisation was hardly much of an improvement on the sanitation of a mediaeval walled city. So she dedicated this work to the great goddess Cloacina, whose function it was to cleanse the drains of the Ancient Rome.

Wilfred Maxwell, a 'wimp' by any standards, learns to assert himself, his creativity and full masculinity under the tutelage of the mysterious Vivien Le Fay Morgan. His asthmatic condition has induced a certain psychism and he has a dream vision at the full moon of his patroness as the High Priestess of the Ancient Moon cult who has returned to calm and control the sea by the house he is now embellishing.

ISBN 1 899585 50 8

THE WINGED BULL A ROMANCE OF MODERN MAGIC

The message of the book concerns the spiritualising of sex. But not the spiritualising of sex by sublimating it onto other planes than the spiritual, but the spiritualising of sex by realising its profound spiritual significance and far-reaching psychological values.

The man whom Ursula Brangwyn loves becomes involved in Black Magic and drags her after him. Her brother, a student of strange arts, knows that the only way he can rescue her is to make her transfer her affections to someone else. He chooses his man and sets to work on his difficult task, making use of certain aspects of the sex relationship that are the carefully guarded secrets of the initiates. The story shows the deliberate building of a curious magnetic rapport between two people who do not attract each other. A highly strung, highly cultured sophisticated girl and an unemployed ex-officer, hard bitten and disillusioned.

ISBN 1 899585 45 1

THE SOCIETY OF THE INNER LIGHT

The Society of the Inner Light is a Society for the study of Metaphysical Religion, Mysticism, and Esoteric Psychology. Their development of their practice.

Its aims are Christian and its methods are Western.

Students can take the Correspondence Course for training in Esoteric Science and developing the daily discipline which can lead to Initiation. Application forms and a copy of the Society's WORK AND AIMS are available from;

>The Secretariat
>The Society of the Inner Light
>38 Steele's Road
>London NW3 4RG
>England
>
>email - sil@innerlight.org.uk